Ignored, Shunned, and Invisible

IGNORED, SHUNNED, AND INVISIBLE

How the Label "Retarded" Has Denied Freedom and Dignity to Millions

J. David Smith

Westport, Connecticut
London

Library of Congress Cataloging-in-Publication Data

Smith, J. David, 1944–
   Ignored, shunned, and invisible : how the label "retarded" has denied freedom
   and dignity to millions / J. David Smith.
     p. cm.
   Includes bibliographical references and index.
   ISBN: 978–0–313–35538–7 (alk. paper)
1. Lovelace, John, 1931–2001. 2. People with mental disabilities—Biography. 3. Mental
retardation facilities patients—Biography. 4. People with mental disabilities—Institutional
care. I. Title.
RC570.2.S63 2009
616.890092——dc22   2008033673

British Library Cataloguing in Publication Data is available.

Library of Congress Catalog Card Number: 2008033673
ISBN-13: 978–0–313–35538–7

First published in 2009

Praeger Publishers, 88 Post Road West, Westport, CT 06881
An imprint of Greenwood Publishing Group, Inc.
www.praeger.com

Printed in the United States of America

∞

The paper used in this book complies with the
Permanent Paper Standard issued by the National
Information Standards Organization (Z39.48–1984).

10 9 8 7 6 5 4 3 2 1

This book is dedicated to the memory of my father, Walter Harrison Smith, Jr.

Contents

Preface

No man is an Iland, intire of it self; every man is a piece of the continent, a part of the main.

—John Donne, *Devotions upon Emergent Occasions*

Historically, segregation and social isolation have been recurring responses to people who are considered defective or deficient in some way. People tend to keep social and physical distance from those they consider to be too different from themselves; too different from the social norms and values they embrace. A society that believes that having a home is essential to normal human life will view homeless people as being deviant, and it will distance them socially from its other members. A society that expects its members to be self-sufficient will look down on and isolate those who are too dependent on others. A society that worships youth will revile old people. A society obsessed with physical and psychological perfection will seek ways to quarantine those who are considered imperfect.

This book is a collection of stories about the struggle that people with the label mental retardation face as they try to connect with the society in which they live, and the reluctance of that society to let them do so. It is also a biography of one man who spent a lifetime on isolated social shores. It is a tale of the ways in which he was often ignored, regularly avoided, and treated as less than a person. The ebb and flow of social policies and practices regarding people with disabilities will be examined through the lens of his life experiences.

The book is also a story of our society, of our parents, friends, and teachers; those who in many cases encouraged us to be kind and generous to others. It is a story about the society that continues to promote values that sometimes inspire us, sometimes challenge us, and sometimes tell us to look the other way when facing unsettling human differences or disturbing human need.

The isolated person, the metaphorical island to which each chapter will return, is John Lovelace. He lived 70 years, and for all of his life his identity was that of a person who was mentally retarded. I use his real name because I hope to reveal, rather than hide, a man who for most of his life was made to be invisible. For John, like others with the label, the risks of visibility are minor compared to the consequences of invisibility and isolation.

JDS

Acknowledgments

Thanks go to my family, friends, and mentors who may read this book and find that their influence in my life has been profound. Thank you for caring about me and believing that I had something of value to say.

Much of the credit for all of my work belongs to my wife, Joyce, and our children Lincoln, Allison, and Sallie. I have been sustained by this love and support over the decades. They have added the greatest richness to my life.

Jennifer Jones has blessed this book with her care and attention to detail. My thanks go also to Natsuko Takemae and Andrea Cox.

Finally, my appreciation goes out to my students, past and present, who have listened to my stories and who have encouraged me to keep telling them.

Introduction
Speaking of Mental Retardation

How does being called mentally retarded influence the feelings and self-esteem of people who are so labeled? Historically, how has it influenced the way that people receiving the diagnosis have been treated? What does it mean for them today? This book presents arguments that the label of mental retardation is and has long been a myth, a myth that possesses destructive power. The evidence offered consists of the voices of people whose lives bear the impact of the retardation designation and who have struggled with the stigma associated with it. Some of the voices are those of fictional characters, their words coming from the insightful observations of acclaimed writers. Others are the words of real people who give voice to their struggles with an identity that is not of their own choosing. In particular, the story of a man named John Lovelace will serve as a personification of the meaning that mental retardation has had in American society.

The stories and voices presented in this book are intended to provoke questions about the meaning of mental retardation, and the people to whom the term and concept is and has been assigned. It is written as an attempt to explain a complex and abstract psychological construct in a manner that does not require prior knowledge, only a willingness to understand the compelling human needs of people who have long been misunderstood.

FORREST: "BEIN A IDIOT"

The 1994 film, *Forrest Gump*, was a humorous and yet moving portrayal of a man who was diagnosed during his early school years as having physical disabilities and an IQ that categorized him as mentally retarded. This highly romanticized saga of life with disabilities unfolds with Forest attending regular public school classes due to the persistence of his mother, becoming a college football star, being decorated as a Vietnam War hero, founding a business that yields millions of dollars, and becoming a spiritual cult figure. Most importantly, it depicts him as a sensitive and strong friend, husband, and father.

The most famous line in the movie appears in the first scene. Forrest offers a chocolate to a nurse sitting next to him at a bus stop. He explains to her, "My momma always said, life is like a box of chocolates. You never know what you're gonna get." In the book by Winston Groom on which the movie was based, however, Forrest's actual reference to a box of chocolates is quite different. It provides a contrasting portrait of his struggle with being classified as retarded.

> Let me say this: bein a idiot is no box of chocolates. People laugh, lose patience, treat you shabby. Now they says folks sposed to be kind to the afflicted, but let me tell you—it ain't always that way. Even so, I got no complaints, cause I reckon I done live a pretty interestin life, so to speak.
>
> I been a idiot since I was born. My IQ is near 70, which qualifies me, so they say. Probly, tho, I'm closer to bein a imbecile or maybe even a moron, but personally, I'd rather think of mysef as like a *halfwit*, or somethin not no idiot—cause when people think of a idiot, more'n likely they be thinkin of one of them Mongolian idiots—the ones with they eyes too close together what look like Chinamen an drool a lot an play with theyselfs.
>
> Now I'm slow—I'll grant you that, but I'm probly a lot brighter than folks think, cause what goes on in my mind is a sight different than what folks see. For instance, I can think things pretty good, but when I got to try sayin or writin them, it kinda come out like jello or something . . .
>
> Now I know somethin bout idiots. Probly the only thing I do know bout, but I done read up on em—all the way from that Doycheeeveskie guy's idiot, to King Lear's fool, an Faulkner's idiot, Benjie, an even ole Boo Radley in *To Kill a Mockingbird*—now he was a *serious* idiot. The one I like best tho is ole Lennie in *Of Mice an Men*. Mos of them writer fellers got it straight—cause their idiots always smarter than people give em credit for. Hell, I'd agree with that. Any idiot would. HeeHee.[1]

DEBORAH OR EMMA? SEARCHING FOR THE TRUE VOICE

In his 1912 book, *The Kallikak Family: A Study in the Heredity of Feeble-mindedness,* the psychologist Henry Goddard portrayed a very real young woman to whom he gave the pseudonym Deborah Kallikak. He presented her as the prototype of his conception of the moron, the term he created for mild mental retardation. He argued that her institutionalization at the Vineland Training School in New Jersey was necessary for her own well-being and for the protection of society. He asserted that if she were released she would almost immediately fall into a life of depravity and promiscuity. He also talked of the institution's positive effects on her life. He included pictures of her in the book that displayed not only her handiwork (sewing and wood-working), but also made evident her physical attractiveness. According to Goddard, she was thriving and growing, in spite of her retardation, because she was institutionalized.

Indeed, Deborah would never be a member of a society other than that of an institution. She was destined to live a total of 81 years in two institutions. From the time she entered the training school until she died at the Vineland State School across the street, she would never know life free of institutional influence. When she died in 1978, she was buried in the institution's cemetery under a marker bearing only her name, her real name: Emma Wolverton.

Descriptions of Deborah subsequent to the publication of the Kallikak study repeatedly refer to her beauty and charm. Edgar Doll worked with Goddard as an assistant from 1912 to 1917, and in 1925 he became director of research at Vineland. In 1983 his son Eugene, who had known Deborah as a child, wrote:

> There is no doubt that, whatever her mentality, she radiated that extra spark of personality which makes one stand out in a crowd and which not only attracts but holds friends. J. . . . E. Wallace Wallin [an eminent American psychologist] wrote urbanely of his first encounter with Deborah—finding her in charge of the kindergarten at the Training School and mistaking her for the teacher. At lunchtime he was surprised to find the same attractive young woman waiting on his table . . .
>
> Time and again visitors in both the Training School and the Vineland State School . . . to which Deborah was later transferred, commented on her seeming normality.[2]

Helen Reeves, executive social worker at the Vineland State School, commented on Deborah's transfer from the training school:

For our part we knew we had acquired distinction in acquiring Deborah Kallikak, for by this time the story of her pedigree was becoming well known. And such an able, well trained and good looking girl must be an asset . . . She excelled in the manual arts of embroidery, woodcraft and basketry, played the cornet beautifully and took star roles in all entertainments as a matter of course. She was well trained in fine laundry work and dining room service, could use a power sewing machine and had given valuable assistance as a helper in cottages for low grade children.[3]

As an adolescent, Deborah served in the home of the superintendent of the Training School. In addition to performing housekeeping duties, she cared for the family's infant son. She later assumed child care responsibilities for the assistant superintendent of the State School. Children from both of these families continued to visit and correspond with Deborah throughout her life. A woman in one of the families acknowledged her affection and respect by naming her own daughter after Deborah.[4]

On occasion, Deborah accompanied the official families to the shore for holidays. Her preference in vacations, however, seems to have been for a series of yearly excursions that she and social worker Reeves took together. Following is Reeves's recollection of their 1939 autumn trip to Washington, D.C.:

As we rolled along southward I did not realize—though I should have—that I was establishing a precedent and that the succeeding five years would find me doing exactly the same sort of thing at this season of the year. Nineteen-forty would see us at the World's Fair in New York City; Luray Caverns would be visited in 1941 and Niagara Falls the year following; New York City again in 1943, and then—gasoline being scarce and travel facilities constricted—1944 would find us in Philadelphia for those three precious days.[5]

Doll quotes one acquaintance as saying, "Hers was a body which moved with full knowledge of the impact of its movements on the opposite sex." He goes on to cite the impression of an employee who had accompanied a group of the institution's girls on a boardwalk stroll: "Every time we passed a man or group of men, they would stop, turn, look after Deborah, and occasionally start to follow us. I do not know what signals Deborah was sending out, but it seemed that one glance from her eyes could summon a following. I was uneasy until we got home, though Deborah had done nothing really fresh or out of order."[6]

While Deborah was serving as a nurse's aide during an epidemic, she stayed in a room near the sick patients. There she was not under the same close supervision as in her usual living area. It appears that her woodworking skill enabled her to alter her window screen for easy exit and entry. She had fallen in love with an employee of the State School (apparently a maintenance worker). They seemingly enjoyed the moonlit grounds and each other in a romantic interlude before being discovered. The young man was "kindly dismissed by a lenient justice-of-the-peace" and regulations were tightened for Deborah.[7] After a similar experience sometime later, Deborah mourned, "It isn't as if I'd done anything really wrong. It was only nature!"[8] Years afterward, she would again fall in love. Helen Reeves provides some insight into the institutional attitude concerning Deborah's feelings of love and her right to romantic involvement.

> In the early fall of 1939 I returned to Vineland after a month's leave to find Deborah's spirits and morale at low ebb. She had worked hard during the summer, trying to do justice to a housework job for one of the official family, keeping on meanwhile with her responsibilities as custodian of the gymnasium and costume room. She had also managed to fall in love while I was away, which romance had been discovered and quietly nipped in full bloom without her knowledge.[9]

How can it be that a woman of considerable talent in several areas of her life, a woman of beauty and charm, a woman lacking in academic skills but able to perform productive work is institutionalized for 81 of the 89 years of her life? When so much of the information that is available indicates that Deborah (Emma) had the potential for living in society, what factors contributed to her lifetime of segregation?

Repeatedly in the accounts of Deborah's life, references are made to her appearance of normality. Visitors and new employees often expressed disbelief when told that she was mentally retarded. Time and again, such skepticism about the validity of classifying Deborah as feebleminded, as a moron, was countered with the results of standardized intelligence tests. Throughout the available reports, her performance on tests of academic or abstract ability was held to be of greater importance than the obvious strengths she demonstrated in her daily life. All subsequent descriptions echo to some degree Goddard's summation of Deborah's condition:

> Here is a child who has been most carefully guarded. She has been persistently trained since she was eight years old, and yet nothing has been accomplished in the direction of higher intelligence or general education. Today if this young woman were to leave the Institution, she would at once become a prey to the designs of evil men or evil women and would lead a life that would be vicious, immoral, or criminal, though because of

her mentality she herself would not be responsible. There is nothing that she might not be led into, because she has no power of control, and all her instincts and appetites are in the direction that would lead to vice.[10]

Goddard eventually tempered his thinking on the issue of the unchangeable nature of mild mental retardation, on the incurability of the moron. Deborah, however, would be affected by the legacy of her original diagnosis for the rest of her life. Perhaps the greatest tragedy was that Deborah came to believe that life in an institution was the only one possible for her. In 1938, she told Helen Reeves, "I guess after all I'm where I belong, I don't like this feebleminded part but anyhow I'm not i-idic like some of the poor things you see around here."[11]

In 1945, Reeves reported that "Deborah, in spite of her conscious superiority, does not feel secure away from the institution . . . The world is a dangerous place, she will tell you."[12]

Deborah was in a wheelchair during her final years. She was often in intense pain because of severe arthritis and was unable to continue the crafts she had loved throughout her life. In her last years, she was offered the alternative of leaving the institution to live in the community she had been denied most of her life. She declined the opportunity. She knew she needed constant medical attention.[13] Emma Wolverton had also come to believe deeply the story that had been told of her in the name of Deborah Kallikak.

The book, *Mother, Can You Hear Me?*, by Elizabeth Cooper is the story of a psychologist who searches for her birth mother. This journey led her to the discovery that her mother was deaf, had been misdiagnosed as mentally retarded, and had been institutionalized. In the book Cooper speaks of her internship in psychology at the Vineland State School and her relationship with Emma Wolverton.

> . . . Sometimes I felt as though I were one of the residents in the small barren institutional room where I spent my nights and several weekends. Emma was one of the residents, and she had interesting stories to tell me. Her job was to do some of the hand ironing, and she had been allowed to set up a small space like a tiny apartment for herself. She was very friendly toward me. From her I learned firsthand about the classic study of two branches of the Kallikak family, from which she was descended . . . She was devoted to the people who conducted the study, as though they were her family. Test results found her to be retarded, but I found her to be informative and interesting to talk with. She was considerate and personable and certainly not what I would think of as a retarded person . . . Emma was tall and reticent in her manner. She reminded me of anyone's elderly aunt . . . The people who [studied] her wanted to show a genetic basis for her mental deficiency.

They traced her roots back to Revolutionary War days—she could have belonged to the D.A.R ... Emma was taken into her training school at an early age and, I believe, "trained" to fulfill the prophecy of deficiency.[14]

Indeed, she had been trained to think of herself as deficient, as retarded—she and thousands of others in America's schools and institutions.

THE STATE SCHOOL BOYS, THE LABEL AND THE REBELLION

Orphaned and then left alone after the death of his foster mother in 1949, eight-year-old Freddie Boyce was given an IQ test. On the basis of this one test score he was sent to the Fernald State School in Massachusetts. He and other children like himself who were diagnosed as having mild mental retardation (feeblemindedness), were denied appropriate educational opportunities and were frequently abused. They were repeatedly told by staff members of the institution that they were incapable and incompetent.

In his book, *The State Boys Rebellion*, Michael D'Antonio describes the humiliation that Freddie, and other boys who had been committed to Fernald under similar circumstances, experienced.

By the time they were 10 or 11, the State Boys understood that nearly everyone on the outside considered them to be "retards." This word hurt them as much as the word "nigger" hurt blacks. When they were angry they flung it at each other.

Attendant James McGinn reduced boys to tears by calling them retards as they waxed the floors and buffed them. More than one would recall, as adults, how McGinn whispered into their ears that they were "worthless" or "stupid" and that "no one gives a shit about you."

Another bit of torture, which McGinn began to use after Freddie had been at the institution for a couple of years, was reserved for those who talked during meals in the downstairs dining room. He would grab a slice of bread from the boy's tray and tear off enough to wad into a ball the size of a large marble. He would then yank the boy to his feet, and tell him to get down on the floor and push the bread with his nose. McGinn would laugh and say, "Look at the retard."[15]

After hearing these words of belittlement and degradation so often from authority figures, some of the boys began to believe they were true.

The humiliation and constant name-calling—retard, lifer, moron—were difficult to ignore. This barrage beat down Albert Gagne until he began to believe that he *was* defective and destined to spend his entire life inside the institution. He became more and more withdrawn from the other boys.[16]

Other boys, however, resisted and challenged the derogatory labels with which they were constantly bombarded. Usually their challenges did not lead to changes in their status, even when the facts uncovered through their challenges belied the names they were being called, and the necessity of their institutionalization. The experience of Joey Almeida illustrates the futility of their efforts.

In a few cases these challenges to the "retarded" label were successful, and the Fernald staff members were forced to recognize that a diagnosis or assessment and classification might be inaccurate. Joey Almeida insisted that his records had his age wrong, that he was really 10 not 11. In a meeting with a social worker, he was so insistent that a mistake had been made that the social worker finally agreed to check his files. It turned out that Joey was right.

Intrigued by the way Joey had calmly asserted himself in conversation, the social worker gave him a new IQ test. In his subsequent report, the social worker wrote that he found "no real evidence of this boy being significantly retarded, particularly to a degree that requires institutionalization." Joey's problem "seems to be emotional rather than his being retarded ... if guided correctly, in a place other than Fernald, he would have a better opportunity in life." Nothing was done in response to this report. Joey remained in Fernald, in the Boys Dormitory, perpetually worried that the daily taunt—you're a lifer— was his fate.[17]

The State Boys were inspired by radio and television reports about the Civil Rights Movement. This led them to protest their verbal and physical abuse by the staff, and even their institutionalization at Fernald. After pleading for better treatment to no avail, they ran away. Caught and brought back, they seized control of their ward and demanded that their rights be recognized. Although they were imprisoned and otherwise punished for their actions, they were eventually released to fend for themselves.

While there were tragic life stories for some of the State Boys, others managed to build strong and productive lives for themselves after leaving Fernald. In the late 1990s they became aware through news coverage that they had been used as human guinea pigs while at the institution. They had been fed radioactive oatmeal as part of an experiment on the physiological effects of radiation. This brought the "boys" together again, and they sued the State of Massachusetts and won a multimillion-dollar settlement.[18]

ESCAPING THE LABEL AT ALL COSTS: THE RAPE AT GLEN RIDGE

In 1989 a group of male high school athletes in the affluent town of Glen Ridge, New Jersey, were accused of sexual assault of another student. She was assaulted with a broom handle, a stick, and a baseball bat. The young woman had been labeled as being mentally retarded. Rape charges were brought against seven of the young men. When the victim was called upon for testimony one of the attorneys defending the accused young men said to her that some people thought of her as having mental retardation. She agreed saying, "Lots of kids in school said that." But she also agreed when the attorney said that she "was proving (herself in court) . . . not retarded." His intent was to show that her performance as a witness was evidence that she was not retarded, and therefore that she had not been taken advantage of by the boys. She provided support for his argument by saying, "If I was retarded, I could never answer all these questions."[19] More important to her than the conviction and punishment of those who had assaulted her was to be seen as competent and articulate. She was driven by the wish to escape the label and to be accepted as a "normal" person.

In spite of her struggle to prove her competence, however, the victim of the Glen Ridge rape remained the person she had been labeled to be in the judgment of the court and others. Expert witnesses, her family, and others who testified portrayed her (in support of the charges against her rapists) as fitting the stereotype of mental retardation. She was described as defective, weak, and unable to protect herself, and so the price of justice in her case was the loss of the identity she craved, to be "normal" instead of "retarded." In the words of one of her convicted abusers, "I now understand . . . how sick she really is, and I just feel great feelings of guilt and shame and I wish nothing had ever happened."[20] Even though her articulate testimony was central to the conviction, she had become to her rapist and others a subject of pity, a person "sick" with retardation.

MENTAL RETARDATION: IT'S LIKE A BOX OF CHOCOLATES. YOU NEVER KNOW WHAT YOU'RE GONNA GET.

In 1992, the American Association on Mental Retardation listed more than 350 conditions in which mental retardation occurs. This list of causes does not, of course, take into account the varying degrees of retardation or other disabilities associated with each of the etiologies.

When those variables are considered, the universe of human conditions subsumed under the term *mental retardation* is overwhelming. The staggering list of causes of mental retardation illustrates the allure and power of typological thinking, which is the belief that complex individual variations can be reduced to underlying human types or essences. Stephen Gelb has found that definitions of mental retardation, regardless of their particulars, are grounded in typological thought.

The term mental retardation has been used to describe people who are more different than they are alike.[21] It has been used as an amalgam for very diverse human conditions. The core of mental retardation as a field is the assumption that somehow there is an "essence" that eclipses all of the differences that characterize people described by the term. It is truly a box of chocolates, however, because "you don't know what you're gonna get" when you reach into the category. Maybe it will be someone who needs constant care, or maybe it will be someone much like yourself but who needs help with academic skills. Perhaps it will be someone with severe physical disabilities, or maybe it will be someone who you would pass on the street without notice.

What is certain about the category is that it is a stigmatizing label with universally negative connotations. That may be the only "glue" that holds it together. According to James Dudley people with the label find that they are not even embraced as part of the disabilities rights movement in the United States. A perspective on the meaning of the term *disability* that has been articulated in recent years is that the definition must be changed in a fundamental way. According to Sarah Triano, a leader in disability rights, "I define disability as a natural and beautiful part of human diversity that people with disabilities can take pride in."[22] Taking pride in one's ability to communicate with sign language or to navigate the environment in a wheelchair can be seen and should be seen as an important part of a person's identity. Listening to the voices of people with the mental retardation label, however, it is hard to imagine how they could see it as "natural and beautiful." Triano, in fact, acknowledges that a person with a "cognitive disability" is likely to be "excluded and left out" of the disabilities rights movement.[23] Speaking of the special difficulties faced by people with mental retardation in becoming part of the movement for self-advocacy and civil rights, she says:

> Hannah Arendt once said that, "the most radical revolutionary will become a conservative the day after the revolution." Since its founding, the disabilities rights movement in the U.S. has served as a strong voice

for radical revolutionary change. But no radical revolutionary force can remain so as long as it refuses to constantly evaluate itself and adapt according to the demands and needs of the changing times. When the strategies we use start to exclude and offend key segments of our community, allow participation by only those privileged members who can afford to participate, and rely on a tactic of secrecy to the point where it becomes an access barrier for members of our community with cognitive and other disabilities, then we have ceased to be radical and revolutionary.[24]

This book is an attempt to understand the evolution and meaning of the concept and terminology of mental retardation. This exploration of mental retardation will be accomplished through the intertwining of two approaches. First, the following chapters will present a story or stories of mental retardation. These are stories intended to show the use and misuse of the diagnosis and the ways in which many people have suffered abuses as a consequence. Second, each chapter will present part of the life story of one man. His name was John Lovelace. His story will be described literally from the day he was born through the day he died. John, who lived with the label of mental retardation for 70 years, illustrates the odyssey through public attitudes, practices, and policies that has been the life course of millions of people with whom he shared its stigma.

CHAPTER 1

What Are You Going to Do About It?

FINDING MYSELF IN JAMAICA

College professors are frequently caricatured as leading lives detached from the realities of the world they study and teach about. They are characterized as living in ivory towers far removed from the everyday realities with which most people must live. This claim may be accurate in some respects. Standing apart from the people, events, and objects that ordinarily surround you may be necessary in order to view most clearly the intellectual, artistic, or social vista you are trying to comprehend. Having spent most of my adult life working in college and university settings, I have had the privilege of doing just that. I have had the luxury of stepping back and taking the time and varied perspectives that have provided me with a richer view of those facets of life that have been the subjects of my inquiries.

This work of observing and reflecting on the social landscape of our culture contrasts sharply with my earlier experiences as a Peace Corps volunteer, public school teacher, and counselor. My experiences as a professor and higher education administrator are also far removed from the intense and constantly demanding work I did with people with disabilities while in high school and college. In addition to enabling me to finance my education, my employment in summer camps for children with disabilities, treatment centers, and hospitals led me to something that came to be for me a special way of making a living.

It gave me a calling, hearing and heeding the voice of meaningful work that the term *vocation* means in literal translation. In places with names like Camp Easter Seal, the Virginia Treatment Center for Children, and the Virginia Home, I came to understand that it is possible to make a direct and positive difference in the lives of people who need help. This was a powerful epiphany for a teenager and young adult who remained immature in many other ways. I also learned that making a difference in the lives of others was gratifying, that it helped bring a new sense of identity to a young person seeking just that.

While my wife, Joyce, and I were serving in the Peace Corps in Jamaica, I discovered that I was drawn to another dimension of human service—assisting people who would help others, thereby amplifying my efforts. Our work with the Ministry of Education in Jamaica fostered in me a sense of the importance of supporting and encouraging teachers, prospective teachers, counselors, and others in the helping professions to become as competent and committed as possible in their efforts to improve the lives of others. During our two years in Jamaica I came to believe that my work in life should somehow continue to involve helping people who, in turn, wanted to help others.

Living in Jamaica taught me another important lesson. While in training for the Peace Corps, we were told that one of the most difficult challenges of our service would be something other than culture shock or matters of diet and physical discomfort. Instead, we were told, one of the most challenging aspects of our service in Jamaica would come after we returned to the United States. We were advised that most people would have difficulty understanding that the Jamaica we had lived in was not the stereotypical tropical paradise that the tourist industry presented to the world. It was likely, we were told, that most people would have problems comprehending why the Peace Corps was needed there at all. Indeed, since our return from Jamaica over 30 years ago, many people have asked how we "lucked out," and whether we enjoyed doing the limbo and scuba diving; some have commented that the rum punch hangovers must have been hell.

Two years of living amid the beauty of that nation's landscape, the kindness of its people, and the charm of its customs was most certainly a pleasure. But Jamaica was also at that time—and remains today—one of the most economically distressed nations in the Western Hemisphere. It continues to struggle for its economic survival and cultural integrity in the world community. I learned much while living there about how little we in the United States understand about the lives of most people in the world. Joyce and I came home having rarely glimpsed the resorts and luxuries that dominate the prevailing image of the country we had learned to love for its sense of pride, purpose, and dignity. We also returned to our own country with a deeper sense of the complexity of the diverse human community we live in and the difficulty that many people have defining their place in it. This sense of connection across human differences has endured for us in our understanding of (and our efforts to better comprehend) everything from the puzzling poverty that is endemic in the United States to the tragedy of international terrorism.

The Peace Corps, Jamaica, graduate school, the beginning of my career as a professor—all of these life markers are a part of my life history now. For many years I taught people who were preparing to become teachers and counselors, or who were otherwise committed to careers in special education, counseling, and rehabilitation. In more recent years I worked as a college and university administrator supporting and encouraging faculty teaching in these disciplines and others. During the journey that has spanned my career I increasingly became part of the higher education establishment. I am vested as a member of the professoriate and still carry with me the perspectives of an administrator. I am concerned, for myself and others, about the practical matters that are of importance to most workers: working conditions, salary, and security. My identity, however, is intimately tied to being an effective teacher, a respected scholar, and a good professional colleague.

I remain convinced that I made the right decision in choosing teaching as a career, and as a way to help my undergraduate and graduate students strengthen both themselves and others. I must admit, however, that the nature of my work has often separated me from the people who are the primary subjects of my teaching, research, and writing: children and adults with disabilities. Although I do not believe that my academic tower is very high or unapproachable, I must acknowledge that I have thrived there. I live with the belief, however, that my work will ultimately prove to have been useful to people with special characteristics and needs.

GOING TO CAMP

I have had several anchors in the "real world" that I think have ensured that academic ivy would not overgrow my genuine perceptions of the realities of the people who I teach and write about. Over the years I have worked as a volunteer in ways that have brought me into regular contact with children and adults with disabilities. I have also frequently visited teachers and other human service professionals in their places of work. These anchors have served to remind me of how difficult it can be to help the people who most need it. They also remind me of how life enhancing this work can be.

My strongest anchor for many years began during my tenure as a professor at Lynchburg College in Virginia. While on the faculty there I regularly worked with my students in organizing and conducting weekend camp retreats for children and adults with the label of mental retardation. Each November and April my students planned and staffed a camping weekend for people with multiple disabilities in addition to mental retardation. There were always new faces among the campers, but we also had a group of "regulars." The same was true of the college students. Some of these undergraduates participated in the camp every semester for four years. Those students who were veterans knew what to expect and often helped the newcomers with their natural anxieties about working with people who were different from themselves in so many ways. They also learned, however, to see the greater human commonalities they shared with them.

The respite weekends were held at Camp Virginia Jaycee, a summer camp facility that serves more than 1,000 children and adults with mental retardation each year. The Camp Jaycee weekends became a tradition at Lynchburg College. As they evolved, the weekends became campus-wide activities, not meant exclusively for special education majors. Throughout the school year students from various majors would engage me in conversations about the experiences of the last camp weekend, and their excitement about the next. More students from majors as diverse as history and business took part each year. To see a math major helping an insecure and intimidated 12-year-old throw a ball or an English major tying the shoes of a 60-year-old man who was unable to do so for himself was extremely gratifying. It was even more gratifying to realize that these acts were performed freely, gladly, and with no promise of reward other than the intrinsic satisfaction of sharing a genuine human exchange of care.

I always returned from those three days feeling good about the relationships I had seen develop between bright young college students with a world of options opening up to them and people whose options were limited by the life circumstances they had been dealt. I also felt privileged to have witnessed what I believed to be the best of what each of those several generations of college students had to offer. Contrary to some of the pessimistic reports and negative opinions concerning college students that have been offered to me during my tenure in higher education, I saw much promise in their futures as compassionate citizen leaders.

I returned from Camp Jaycee in April 1987 feeling, as usual, warmed and optimistic. I was also extremely troubled by one aspect of our weekend. The event that had disturbed and challenged me was the same one that had introduced me to a man named John Lovelace. This event would lead me to become involved in John's life in a way I could not have anticipated at the time. That weekend changed my life in a very fundamental sense. It may also have changed John's life in small way. The greater impact and benefit of the relationship that began during that weekend, however, was on my life.

My students and I always departed for Camp Jaycee early on Friday afternoon, arriving at the camp around two o'clock. The camp is located about an hour's drive from Lynchburg and is nestled in a beautiful valley at the foot of the Blue Ridge Mountains near Roanoke. After making cabin assignments and unpacking, the students, now beginning to think of themselves as counselors, gathered in the dining hall. After a few words of orientation from me, they met in cabin groups to go over the application materials for each camper. They worked with intensity since the campers would start arriving shortly, around four o'clock. Included in each application was information on the camper's medications, disabilities, and special needs.

MEETING JOHN LOVELACE

In April 1987 an unusual question was raised concerning the application materials for John Lovelace, a camper who was about to arrive. Included in his file was a medical consultation form that I now believe had been included by mistake when his application was submitted by the adult home where he then lived. John was 56 years old that spring and living in the Burrell Home for Adults in Roanoke. Burrell housed nearly 200 people—people later described to me as "dead-end" people. They were mostly poor, sick, old, severely disabled, alone in life, and usually some combination thereof. The building itself was a tragic anachronism. In the 1950s it had been the segregationist hospital for African American people in Roanoke. In the 1980s it was still an instrument of segregation, its residents pariahs not because of race but because they could claim no other place in a society in which they were only marginal citizens.

The medical consultation form attached to John's application had been prepared a week earlier. It included the following notations:

A. *Vascular anomaly*

B. 1. *Not a surgical candidate*

   2. *No code*

   3. *Do not resuscitate in the event of cardiac arrest*

The form was brought to my attention by Ev Werness, the executive director of Camp Jaycee. He handed me the form and asked what I thought it should mean for John's weekend stay. I was immediately disturbed by the larger implications of the directive's wording. For the moment, however, I focused my attention on Ev's concern. We discussed it briefly and immediately agreed that we would not honor the no-code order. We decided that if there was a medical crisis involving John he would receive the same emergency treatment that would be provided for anyone else. We shared this decision with the camp nurse and we all agreed that in an emergency every life-sustaining measure would be used.

Two other notes on John's medical consultation form struck me as important. The first indicated that he had no next of kin, and the other stated that he "maintains his own personal affairs." These comments led me to suspect that he had been asked to agree with the no-code order—that he had been treated as a competent adult in that decision, with no need for a guardian or other advocate. My hunch would later prove to be correct.

Friday evenings at Camp Jaycee were always joyful. The main event was a dance that lured even the most timid camper or nervous college student onto the floor. It was so much fun that everything else was lost in the music and movement. For a little while I almost forgot the no-code order. John Lovelace danced much of the night away with counselors and other campers. He smiled and laughed without interruption.

After the dance was over and the campers were safely in bed, most of my students gathered back in the dining hall to talk about the events of the day, and to plan for Saturday. This was always a period of emotional release, with students who had doubts about themselves and their experiences earlier in the day often finding new self-confidence and asking a torrent of questions about the campers: Why does he do this? Why is she afraid of that? Do you think she understands? What should I do if . . . ? Often questions arose that I couldn't answer to the satisfaction of my students. One of those was asked on that Friday night in April 1987.

Earlier in the day I had spoken with a few of the students about John and the no-code order. They talked with others, and now there was widespread interest among them in knowing more about both John and the order. I talked with them about the meaning of the no-code order—no treatment to sustain life in a threatening physical crisis. I also explained the reasoning behind such an order—the quality of the person's life does not justify saving it. We compared John with other people who might be assigned the order—someone in a chronic comatose state, for example, or someone with an irreversible degenerative disease suffering from severe, irremediable pain. John did not fit with these scenarios. He had intellectual and social disabilities, but he was actively engaged with others and clearly derived enjoyment from being alive. He was ambulatory and communicative and he was not chronically ill.

"WHAT ARE YOU GOING TO DO ABOUT IT?"

My students wanted to know why John had been "written off." I could only speculate at that point, of course. I asked them to think about what attributes, other than the label of mental retardation, might have made John vulnerable to the order. They offered profound insights. He was poor. He was alone in life and, therefore, had no family or other natural advocates. He was at-risk for being viewed as a "surplus person," as a non-contributing member of society. These factors were considered cumulatively by my students, and this led them to conclude that he was an unlikely candidate for emergency intervention given the prevailing values of our culture: John was expendable.

As a follow-up to their analysis and conclusions I discussed with them the idea that people with mental retardation have not escaped the prejudices of the past. The failure to recognize them as fully human is not an artifact of history. The struggle for the total citizenship of people with disabilities continues today. I concluded my comments (sermon?) by encouraging them to be part of the struggle for the civil rights of these people.

At that point in our conversation I was feeling very good about what I had said to them and about their evident and impressive comprehension of the issues that John's circumstances presented to us. I was, in fact, glad that John's plight had come to our attention. It had, after all, proved to be a gripping lesson for all of us.

Then came *the* question. I was prepared for more questions about mental retardation and about the social, medical, and psychological meaning of the concept. The question that came, however, cut straight to the fabric of my own values and ethics. It came from a student who for several months had been listening to me lecture on the critical need for advocacy and activism on behalf of people who have disabilities. At the end of my commentary on John Lovelace, she looked me straight in the eyes and, with trust and sincerity, asked, "Dr. Smith, what are you going to do about it?"

Her question was not a challenge; it was the question of a concerned 20-year-old who believed I could make a difference. The direct and authentic character of her trust shook me. I was also intimidated, almost frightened, by her assumption that I was both sufficiently committed and capable of doing something that would make a significant difference in John's life.

How I wished at that moment for some bold and definitive response to her question. In fact, I had nothing to offer her and the other students. The best I could do at that moment was to say that I wasn't sure just what could be done. I mumbled something about having to be careful with confidential information and not wanting to do anything that could hurt the chances for John and other campers coming to subsequent Camp Jaycee weekends. I closed saying, however, that I would look into the matter further.

The rest of the weekend went well. All of my students, particularly those in his cabin, showered John with praise and encouragement for even the smallest accomplishment in arts and crafts, sports, and music. He responded with laughter and with a huge appetite both for the camp food and for the attention he was receiving. In their relatively untutored wisdom the students treated him as a fellow human who deserved recognition of his dignity and compassion for his needs. There were no further questions asked of me about John and his future.

We returned to the college exhausted but gratified. In my mind, however, the question kept echoing: "Dr. Smith, what are you going to do about it?"

CHAPTER 2

Minimally Decent Samaritans

ALLISON'S QUESTION

"Daddy, what are you going to do about it?" This is the question that was asked of me the previous summer by my seven-year-old daughter Allison. We were vacationing in New York City. Joyce and I were excited about introducing our children to the city where we had lived while studying and working at Columbia University. We treasured the memories of our years there, and we wanted to revisit them with nine-year-old Link, seven-year-old Allison and five-year-old Sallie.

In the decade since we had lived there, however, New York City had faced greater challenges. Changes in governmental policies and programs had manifested themselves most visibly among the urban poor. There were more homeless, confused, and disenfranchised people on the streets of New York than we had ever seen. Our children knew the term *street people* only as an abstraction. Now, as we walked the streets of Manhattan, they connected that term with the real people they saw sleeping on the pavement, rummaging through garbage, or walking about disoriented and dirty.

Allison was particularly moved by what she saw, and she asked if I thought a man who looked alarmingly ill and exhausted would die. I answered that unless something happened—unless he got help—he probably would. That was when she asked what I have come to call "Allison's question."

Joyce and I, like most parents, tried to teach our children to do the "right thing" in relation to other people. Again, like most other parents, we tried to teach them by example that other people should be treated with care and respect, and so I took Allison's question as a positive sign: she had come to expect her parents to help other people when they needed it. At age seven, however, she also believed that we had the ability to do whatever was needed to help others, and with immediacy. She trusted that we could always "make things better."

On the street in New York, I was awkward and inarticulate in answering Allison's question, much as I would be later with my student's question about John Lovelace. As I stumbled and stammered my way around Allison's query, the best I could do was talk about not being able to help everyone in need in every situation, and immediately. I talked about how our contributions to charities and voluntary organizations helped people like the man she was asking about. I talked about how some of our taxes were used to help them, and that her mother and I believed that was a very good thing. She was not satisfied with my answer. I was silent in my embarrassment to have offered it to my child. The moment passed but my discomfort did not.

In the biblical story of the Good Samaritan, the two men who passed by the sufferer without helping him crossed to the far side of the road as they passed. Not only did they refuse to help, they also avoided as completely as possible being near the victim of suffering. These men were probably not unfeeling and inhumane. They simply would not or could not risk becoming involved. Perhaps they were family men with responsibilities to others that took precedence in their decision to avoid being involved with the unfortunate man lying by the road. Perhaps they were afraid of being tricked and becoming victims themselves of attack and robbery. Maybe they were afraid of becoming involved with someone who would require more and more of them; more than they could give. And so, they walked to the other side of the road to avoid seeing more clearly and closely the hurts and needs of the man whom they felt they could not risk helping.

It was months before I spoke again with Allison about her question. Finally I found a way of talking with her about the limits of what one person can do for all of those who need help. In addition to talking with her about the parable of the Good Samaritan, I explained to Allison that although her mother and I could not help everyone who needed help, we cared. I told her that even though seeing a need you can't help is painful, we must always look directly at the needs of others, and care about them. I also told her that I believed the words

"I don't care" are among the saddest words that people speak. Using the parable again, I explained that what is most important is that we not walk to the other side of the road. We talked a bit longer, and I believe she understood what I was trying to say.

ANSWERING THE QUESTION

I came close to telling my students something similar in regard to John Lovelace; we can do nothing to substantially change John's situation but we can—should—be sensitized by our knowledge of it. Just knowing of the no-code decision regarding John, I reasoned, could make us more aware of the very little value that our society places on the lives of people with mental retardation. Hopefully this would inspire and energize us to make a difference when and where we could. I came close to leaving it at that.

Before I proceed further with this story it is important that I provide a disclaimer to the reader. Please understand that nowhere in this story should my efforts on John's behalf be considered extraordinary in any way. There is one hero in this story; John Lovelace was heroic in his psychological and social survival for many years against staggering odds. I received more through my relationship with him than I gave to it. This will become increasingly evident later.

Decades ago the philosopher Judith Jarvis Thomson, in discussing the murder of Kitty Genovese in New York City, revisited the parable of the Good Samaritan. Kitty Genovese was murdered—through repeated attacks—while 38 people watched from their apartment windows and did nothing to help her. Thomson pointed out that a truly good Samaritan, true to the parable, would have rushed down to the street, risking death in an effort to help. Such a person, she said, would be not just good, but more. That person would be, in Thomson's words, a Splendid Samaritan! In fact, however, not one of the 38 witnesses even picked up a telephone to call the police, an action that would have caused no danger for them. Calling the police, Thomson said, would have been the act of a Minimally Decent Samaritan.[1] What we need to make a more decent society is not a few Splendid Samaritans but millions of Minimally Decent Samaritans. There may even be one or a few moments in a lifetime for some people to be Splendid Samaritans, and those moments may become the stuff of legend or news accounts. These are heroic and admirable acts. We need more acutely, however, the day-to-day caring of the Minimal Decent Samaritans. It is that quality of character in ourselves and others that makes for a more decent society.

Bottom line: The confidence and trust of that student proved to be too much for me to allow John's story to be just an example cited in a lecture. I decided to take at least one small step closer to the realities of John's life, even if it meant seeing a hurt more clearly and still being unable to make a difference. I decided to make what I thought would be a minimally decent inquiry on his behalf. On Monday morning after the camp weekend I wrote to the Burrell Home for Adults, addressing my letter to the social worker who had arranged for John to come to Camp Jaycee. From her comments on the camp application she had completed for John she appeared to be taking a personal interest in him. I wrote her as follows:

> First let me introduce myself. I am a professor at Lynchburg College. Each semester I take a group of students to Camp Virginia Jaycee for a weekend. These students, special education majors, nursing majors, and others who are interested, serve as counselors for the respite weekends of which you are aware. I have been taking students to Camp Virginia Jaycee for more than a decade.
>
> This past weekend some information which puzzles me concerning one of your residents who attended the camping weekend came to my attention. Included with the information on John Lovelace was a medical consultation form. The date of the consultation was 3/24/87. The consultation appears to have been a follow-up on John's recent illness with flu. Under the heading of "Recommendations" are the following statements:

> A. Vascular anomaly
> B. 1. Not a surgical candidate
>   2. No code
>   3. Tinker Mountain [a sheltered workshop]
>   Do not resuscitate in the event of cardiac arrest

> I find these statements most disturbing. I am asking for your help in understanding these recommendations. I noticed on the consultation form that John has no next of kin. I assume that you are the person who knows most about him. That is why I am writing to you for help in understanding this matter. Will you help me with this?
>
> Thanks in advance for your assistance. Please let me know if you have any questions.

The next Thursday I received a call from John's social worker. She was pleasant and helpful given the conditions of our conversation; confidentiality concerns placed limits on what she could discuss with me. However, she was able to confirm my hunch that even though John had spent many years in a mental retardation institution, he had never been declared incompetent and, therefore, had never been assigned a legal guardian. Though unable to elaborate, she also confirmed that John had participated in the no-code decision as a legally competent party representing himself. I asked her if the vascular anomaly mentioned on the consultation form was an uncorrectable condition that could potentially create a life-threatening crisis. She could not comment on this in any detail, but she shared my impression that this was the case.

The only way that I could look more closely into John's situation appeared to be with legal assistance. The Virginia Department for the Rights of the Disabled seemed to me to be a sensible place to start. Later on the same day that I spoke with John's social worker I wrote to Susan Spielberg at the Department:

> Dear Ms. Spielberg:
>
> I attended the session that you and your associates conducted at Virginia Tech in September and was most impressed. I now have the need to call upon your expertise in a more direct manner.
>
> The enclosed copy of a letter I wrote recently will indicate to you that I am concerned for the well-being of a 56-year-old mentally retarded man. The information I cite in the letter to his social worker will indicate to you that I am concerned as to whether the best interests of John Lovelace are being protected. By the way, John is completely ambulatory, has all the basic self-help skills, and thoroughly enjoyed the camping weekend I refer to in the letter . . .
>
> I received a call this morning from [the social worker] which was most helpful. Although our conversation was limited by the confidentiality of the matter, she explained to me that John has never been declared incompetent and, therefore, does not have a legal guardian. Because of his circumstance, John apparently participated in the "no code" decision. I would question whether he is actually capable of a decision of that magnitude. [She] did indicate that his vascular condition is considered inoperable.
>
> I would appreciate hearing from you with any opinions or advice you may have to offer. Thanks very much for considering my request. Please let me know if you have any questions.

Susan responded promptly to my request for assistance, expressing agreement with my concern over John's ability to give informed consent in a matter of such gravity and indicating that she had already assigned a staff attorney to assist me in exploring the questions I had raised.

The attorney contacted me right away and, after we discussed John's situation briefly, she gave me an assignment. She would be sending the appropriate consent forms to me. I would take them to Roanoke, I would ask John to sign them, and, if he did so, return them to her. She would then start the process of obtaining the records that would tell us more about John's circumstances. She also asked for the names and addresses of people from whom the necessary records could be requested.

On the first Monday in May I wrote to her explaining:

> I visited John Lovelace at the Burrell Home for Adults in Roanoke yesterday. I read the consent form to him and explained it as best I could. He signed it with no hesitation. He executed this signature with great effort and care. It is not very clear but it is genuinely his and I expect is typical of the way he signs his name.
>
> I hope that you will find the form to be in proper order and ready to use. I am anxious to see what John's records can tell us. It seems to me that the basic questions we should be seeking to answer at this point are:

1. What is the exact nature of John's "vascular anomaly?" What is the usual correction for this condition? Why has John's condition not been treated?

2. Why is John "not a surgical candidate?" What is the significance of his financial situation in this designation? Did his having "no next of kin" influence this decision?

3. How was the "no-code—do not resuscitate" decision made? Did John participate in this decision? Is he truly competent to make such a decision? Is this decision actually in his best interest?

> These are the kinds of questions that have been driving my concern for John's welfare. I offer them to you for refinement in relation to the legal structure. I look forward to your opinions on these matters.

I followed this letter with another suggesting possible sources of information for the attorney to pursue. I recommended that she contact the physician who had issued the no-code order and, of course, the Burrell Home administration. I also suggested that she try the Mental Health and Mental Retardation Services office in Roanoke. By this time I had located and spoken with the social worker who worked with John when he lived at an institution that was now called the Central Virginia Training Center. She seemed to remember John well. I felt that, released from confidentiality constraints by the consent form, she could probably provide important insights on what John's life was like while he was in the institution. That might, in turn, help to illuminate his present circumstances. Soon after passing this information on to the attorney, however, I felt a growing need to know more about John's life for myself, and I began my own search to retrieve his history for both of us:for John because he was entitled to his heritage, and for me because I needed to understand how a human life can come to be so devalued by its own society. And so I asked John to sign another consent form, one that would open his files at the Central Virginia Training Center to me. I also began to examine courthouse documents and newspaper archives in the town where he was born. While waiting for the attorney's assistance in understanding what had happened at the Burrell Home, I began to piece John's life story together.

CHAPTER 3

Feebleminded
John Lovelace, Patient #6839

THE STERILIZATION OF CARRIE BUCK

In 1927, a young woman named Carrie Buck was involuntarily sterilized by the Commonwealth of Virginia. She was the first person subjected to that surgery under a state law that had been declared constitutional by the U.S. Supreme Court earlier that year. It provided the legal authority for states to sterilize men and women who were judged to be psychologically or socially incompetent, and who were considered likely to genetically transmit their "deficiencies" to their offspring. Carrie Buck had been committed to an institution and diagnosed as "feebleminded." Her institutionalization followed the birth of an illegitimate daughter.

After Carrie's operation, thousands of other people were sterilized under the Supreme Court's sanction. A conservative estimate is that in the United States 50,000 people were involuntarily sterilized. The Supreme Court's legal model was used six years later by the Nazi regime as part of the so-called race hygiene program. In 1933, the same sterilization statute that had been enacted by the Virginia legislature became law in Germany.

The Nazi law was implemented swiftly. By the end of the first year that it was in force, more than 56,000 people had been judged defective and were then sterilized. Between 1933 and 1945, 2 million people were sterilized under the German law.[1] In *Mein Kampf,* Adolph Hitler, discussing eugenics, argued that

> ... the right of personal freedom recedes before the duty to preserve the race. The demand that defective people be prevented from propagating equally defective offspring is a demand of the clearest reason and if systematically executed represents the most humane act of mankind.[2]

Eugenicists believed that complex human characteristics were often the products of single genes, which they referred to as "unit traits." They held that single-gene determination was true not only of physical traits like eye color and height but also of complex personality and intellectual attributes. Belief in genetic determinism was extended to occupational preferences, academic interests, talents, and even character strengths and weaknesses. Such simplistic views about human nature were inherent in the conviction that sterilization would help stem the feared flood of incompetence resulting from a perceived genetic blight. These views were used to stereotype entire classes of people according to prevailing racial, ethnic, and socioeconomic biases.

It was on the basis of these beliefs and this reasoning that Carrie Buck was sterilized. The eugenic arguments in Carrie's case were, however, inaccurate. Carrie's child, alleged to represent the "third generation of imbeciles" in her family, actually grew to be an honor roll student. After her sterilization Carrie was released to a mountain village, where she later married the deputy sheriff. She lived a modest but productive and respectable life. Friends and employers attested to the fact that Carrie was a competent and caring person. Indeed, mental health professionals who observed her late in her life found no evidence of intellectual disability. If the eugenics researchers in her case had looked just two more branchings back on her family tree, they would have discovered that her grandfather and great-grandfather in the Buck line were both prosperous farmers. Analysis of another branching back would have revealed the ironic likelihood that she was descended from one of the most prominent families in Virginia's history.[3]

Carrie Buck's story is a tragic saga of an injured life as well as an important illustration of the allure and danger of accepting simple answers to complex human questions. The lawyers, physicians, scientists, and politicians involved with the case were not sinister figures. They were convinced that they were serving the best interests of society through their actions. They advanced a scientific and political agenda that they felt would lead to the eradication of social problems and the prevention of suffering. They were wrong, however, and their mistake bore tragic results for untold numbers of people throughout the world, including John Lovelace and his mother Etta.

THE STERILIZATION OF ETTA LOVELACE

On May 26, 1931, a 19-year-old woman was unofficially committed to Western State Hospital in Staunton, Virginia. It was unofficial because she was not retained in the institution at that time. She was, using the institutional term, "furloughed" until the legal paperwork could be completed to allow the hospital to perform the surgical procedure on her that was the actual reason for her commitment: sterilization.

The young woman's name was Etta Virginia Lovelace. According to her commitment papers, hospitalization at Western State was necessary because of "immoral conduct and sexual promiscuity." Her records also indicated that she had recently given birth to an illegitimate child. She was described as having been "feebleminded since birth; mother and father were also feebleminded." There was no elaboration or substantiation for this diagnosis in her records. It is interesting to note that she had been assigned the diagnosis of feeblemindedness, and that situated between her home in Martinsville, Virginia, and Western State Hospital in Staunton, an institution for "mentally ill" people, was the institution then known as the Virginia Colony for Feebleminded and Epileptics. I believe this is an indication that in the eugenic frenzy of the time, sterilization was the real goal in institutionalizing thousands of people like Etta Lovelace. The particulars of diagnostic classification and appropriate placement and treatment were largely irrelevant.

On June 29, 1931, Etta returned to the hospital from her "furlough" in preparation for her sterilization. Apparently the necessary legal documents had been fully processed by that time. It was noted in her records that she made a good adjustment to the hospital routine and "helped a great deal on the ward." Her hospital records indicate that she was sterilized on November 1, 1931. It is stated that she "made an uneventful postoperative recovery."

Although the purpose of her institutionalization was clearly sterilization, Etta Lovelace was to live in the institution for almost two years. The hospital records do not indicate any reason for her being held that long. My sense is that she was there for such an extended period simply because of the slowness of action in the large state hospital bureaucracy. Apparently during those two years no psychological testing was done that might have supported the legitimacy of her diagnosis as feebleminded. Notes under the title of "Formal Mental Examination" offer some insights, however, concerning what this young woman was like:

> ...she was cooperative and attentive. Answered questions to the best of her ability. She gave a history of having had one illegitimate child which had been taken from her by a minister in her community. She did not object to the operation for sterilization. She was able to do simple counting and calculation, but was unable to read, but could write her name. She had worked successfully as a housekeeper in various homes prior to admission. She had been arrested on one occasion for vagrancy. She said that this was due to her inability to get a job where she could stay in the house, and she had no place to go.

On the basis of not being able to read, having an illegitimate child, and being poor, Etta Lovelace was diagnosed as feebleminded. Her discharge indicated that she was unimproved. Her formal diagnosis was "Without psychosis, Mental deficiency, Moron."

Moron was the term used at the time for people who were thought to be "high grade defectives." These were individuals judged to be mentally retarded but who did not show clear signs of head injury, malformation, or disease. They were thought to be retarded because of genetic weakness—they were from "poor stock," the result of the "bad seed," the inheritors of insufficient intelligence to cope with normal social demands. They were also thought to be highly prone to criminal behavior, immorality, and promiscuity. Much of what was done in the name of expanding the number and size of residential institutions and the implementation of involuntary sterilization practices during the first half of the twentieth century was actually aimed at this group.

Even a brief study of what occurred in the field of mental retardation during this period, however, makes it clear that those who were diagnosed as morons, then institutionalized and sterilized, were poor, uneducated people who for one reason or another were considered to be problematic by those in powerful and authoritative positions. They were judged to be misfits who should be removed from their home communities. It is also clear that the men and women who were institutionalized and sterilized during this period tended to be people who had no family or friends with the power to help them, nor the resources to help themselves. Etta Lovelace, unfortunately, fit this profile all too perfectly.

When she was admitted to Western State Hospital Etta was given a physical examination. She was described as being 5 feet, 6 inches tall and weighing 140 pounds. She had brown hair and blue eyes. She was in good health. Her health was not a problem, but her life situation was. She was impoverished and illiterate. She was perceived to be a problem because of her socially unacceptable behavior in a small Virginia town. She had no advocates. When she was interviewed upon admission she told the interviewer that she made her living doing housework. She was quizzed about this, and the questions posed to her were underlined in the hospital record. She responded as follows:

> . . . What did you do in the house?
> Cleaned up and cooked, and washed.
> What did you cook?
> Anything I could get hold of.
> Can you cook beans?
> Yes.
> How?
> Wash them nice and clean, and put water and salt and a piece of meat in them.
> How long does it take to cook them?
> I put them on at nine o'clock and they are done by 10 . . .
> Can you make biscuits?
> Yes.
> How?
> Cut them out.
> What do you put in them?
> Soda, sometimes baking powders, and milk.
> What sort of milk?
> Butter milk . . .
> How do you make corn bread?
> I take two eggs and milk and a little soda and salt.
> What do you do besides cooking?
> Nothing but work on the farm. I shucked corn and suckered tobacco
> . . .
> Did you ever have any children?
> One.
> Is it alive?
> Yes . . .
> How old is the baby?
> It was born last year at the time we shucked corn.
> Who is looking after the child?
> A preacher took him away from me.

Do you nurse the baby?
Feed him on the bottle.
You have just had one?
Yes.
Were you willing to come and stay here for us to help you and do what
we can for you?
I would rather stay at home.

JOHN LOVELACE: BECOMING PATIENT #6839

And so the story of John Lovelace's life begins to take form. He was
born to Etta but was soon taken from her. She was shortly thereafter
institutionalized and sterilized. After two years she returned to her
home in Martinsville, but she would never reestablish a parental relationship with her son. He would subsequently know about her, but he
would never know her as his mother.

A 1946 physician's report sheds some light on John's early life after
he was taken from Etta:

> ...The Salvation Army was looking for a temporary home in which to
> place the child. They placed the baby with this family and never made
> arrangements to take him out. Consequently, he has been with them
> without adoption all of his life. They have treated him as their own child.
> The foster-mother had been married before and had a daughter, who
> now has children. When the child was six months old his eyes and
> mouth drew over to the right, and he had "drawing" spells, in which
> his head and heels almost touched. These would last for an hour or
> more. They continued for two weeks. He was taken to Dr. Newman in
> Danville, who determined that he had syphilis and treated him. This
> helped a great deal, but the boy has never been right. They put him in
> school, and the teacher frankly told the foster-mother that he couldn't
> learn. The foster-mother tried to teach him herself, but she found out that
> it was impossible.

When John was 16 his foster parents became worried about his
behavior. There seem to have been concerns about some peculiarities
in his behavior, but more troubling, however, were his temper tan-
trums. The same physician included in his report the following comments from John's foster parents:

> The main concern now is that during the past year he has had an in-
> crease in his rages. They have become more violent. He is very cruel to
> the animals, and on one occasion he attacked his foster-mother with
> pitchfork and a knife. He has had periods when he eats ravenously,

and then periods when he will go without anything. He has begun to masturbate. He will play well with the foster-mother's grandchildren for several hours and then will become irritated with them. He will have periods of being fractious, and if his foster-mother does not appear to pay attention to them, they disappear and he seems to repent. He makes a great deal of noise sleeping.

Some of these characteristics would not seem to be very unusual for a 16-year-old boy. Others would be signs of a young man experiencing frustration and turmoil in his life. The physician went on to describe John's physical disabilities and apparent mental retardation. He said that John walked with a limp on his right side, that his speech was impaired, and that his mental abilities were seen as limited. His reflexes were described as slow.

John's "virtues" were delineated as being "good at milking" and doing work in the family's garden. He apparently was also helpful in other ways on the farm.

Even though he had "virtues," John's difficulties continued to over-shadow them. His troubles led to his being institutionalized two years later when he was 18. John was committed to what was by then referred to as the Lynchburg State Colony. As mentioned previously, that institution was officially titled the Virginia Colony for Feeble-minded and Epileptics. It has since been called the Lynchburg Train-ing School and Hospital and, most recently, the Central Virginia Training Center. For many years it was the largest residential facility in the United States for people diagnosed as mentally retarded. It was the place where the Carrie Buck case was initiated, and it was there that she was sterilized following the Supreme Court's 1927 decision.

John was committed in October of 1948. As part of that process a social worker from Martinsville sent a letter to the Colony with infor-mation about John's home life. Her comments are very illuminating of the environment in which John grew up. They also provide more detail on the difficulties that he had been having:

> We talked with Mr. and Mrs. W. I. Hunter, foster parents of the above named child. The Hunters live in a very cheap mill section and have a very small home. The house is very sparsely furnished, but immacu-lately kept. It was rather early in the morning when the [social] worker called, but even at that hour the house was spotless, as well as Mr. and Mrs. Hunter and John. Both the parents gave the worker the impression of being honest and sincere.

Mr. and Mrs. Hunter were attending a Salvation Army meeting about eighteen years ago and were asked to take a baby and keep it for ten days until a permanent home could be found ... When they took the baby, all they knew about his background was that his mother was unmarried. Later they found that she was not normal mentally. Since then they have also met several of his aunts and from what they say, feeblemindedness is a strong family characteristic. The child was taken to Dr. Newman, Pediatrician, Danville, Virginia, who gave him shots for syphilis. When John was six months old he had infantile paralysis. This affected his right side. He was almost four years old before he began to talk or walk. Over the period of eighteen years, the Hunters have carried John from first one doctor to another, with the hope that something might be done for him.

In 1945 he was examined at the University of Virginia Hospital, Charlottesville, Virginia. For the last three or four weeks the boy has been having a very severe headache every day. These headaches lasted for a very short while. It seems that John is very calm and harmless until his blood pressure goes up. Mrs. Hunter says that when this happens he becomes very angry and seems to want to hurt something.

The social worker's statement gives a portrait of a caring couple with limited resources who had invested much of their lives in a child with exceptional needs. It etches a wonderful picture of people willing to give generously to a child who desperately needed to be accepted and cared about. It also shows that they had reached the limits of their abilities to help and understand him. In 1948 there was no help available to them outside the institution to which they sent their son. There was simply nowhere else for them to turn for assistance.

The statement also illustrates the conflicting opinions and interpretations of the sources of John's disabilities. Congenital syphilis was again mentioned as a reason for his problems. Polio (infantile paralysis) is introduced as a reason for the physical limitations on the right side of his body. Finally, the genetic quality of his heritage is questioned, with the opinion being conveyed that his mother and her sisters were of "feebleminded stock," with the implication that this might explain John's difficulties. Each of these explanations emerged again and again as John's life was woven in and out of the social institutions that were controlling his destiny.

In October 1948 John Richard Lovelace became Patient 6839 at the Lynchburg State Colony. On his fourth day in residence there he was seen for a psychological evaluation. The psychologist concluded his report with the following observations:

Despite the fact that the family from which he is derived is filled with incidence of mental deficiency, it appears that the diagnosis will have to be a toss-up between birth injury or congenital lues [congenital syphilis].

Recommendation:

Sterilization seems to be feasible since his foster-parents are anxious for him to be furloughed for short periods of time. He is given to too much agitation and is too low grade to profit from any school. Simple training in manual tasks combined with recreational therapy are about all that can be offered.

CHAPTER 4

"Patient Is Full Code"

SIMPLE SIMON

In his book, *Inventing the Feeble Mind*, James Trent examined the history of changes in the meaning of mental retardation in the United States. He began his examination with Simple Simon, the nursery rhyme. The rhyme first became popular during the postrevolutionary period and it illustrated, Trent said, that people thought of as simpletons were ridiculed and teased but not feared. Trent reported, in fact, that simpletons were a known and expected part of the farm and village life of early American culture.[1]

> Simple Simon met a pieman
> Going to the fair;
> Says Simple Simon to the pieman,
> "Let me taste your ware."
> Says the pieman to Simple Simon
> "Show me first your penny."
> Says Simple Simon to the pieman,
> "Indeed I have not any."
> Simple Simon went a-fishing,
> For to catch a whale;
> All the water he had got
> Was in his mother's pail.
> Simple Simon went to look
> If plums grew on a thistle;

He pricked his fingers very much,
Which made poor Simon whistle.
He went for water in a sieve,
But soon it all ran through.
And now poor Simple Simon
Bids you all adieu.[2]

As life in the United States became more urban and industrial, the image of the simpleton was transformed and subdivided into the idiot, the imbecile, and, eventually, the moron categories. The moron was considered the "high-grade" defective, with imbeciles and idiots occupying lower steps on the mental continuum, respectively. The idiot was diagnosed by the inability to speak, and the imbecile could speak but was clearly incapable of transcending a childlike state. The moron was considered most dangerous because this person often escaped notice during childhood and adolescence and became an irresponsible and antisocial adult. These forms and levels of what was known as feeblemindedness implied pathology and required containment. That containment was provided through the social and political creation of residential institutions. Institutions as the appropriate place for people diagnosed as being mentally retarded came to dominate the public understanding of them for many decades.

CONSTRUCTING MENTAL RETARDATION

Trent argued that mental retardation was constructed within the context of the residential institution for different reasons and with varying meanings. At times retardation was defined in the name of science, for the purpose of understanding its causes and possible prevention. At other times mental retardation was defined and classified in the name of care. Where was the best place for people so classified, and how could they best be treated? In other instances mental retardation was defined in the name of social control. How can society best be protected from the ills these people create? He found that the goals of care and control were often commingled in the missions of institutions. What was provided as care for people who were judged not able to adequately manage for themselves was also rationalized as being of service to society. It provided economic and social protection. Trent observed, however, that what was done in the name of care and protection often diminished the resources, status, and power of institutionalized people. By being institutionalized their economic and social potentials receded; they became dependent and powerless primarily because of their institutionalization rather than retardation.

In *Abandoned to Their Fate,* Philip Ferguson spoke of mental retardation from another perspective. He described the impact of the judgment of chronicity on the lives of people considered to be retarded. Through his study of mental retardation in the nineteenth and early twentieth century, Ferguson found that to be judged "chronic" meant to be socially abandoned. In Ferguson's words, the judgment of chronicity is reached when "badness becomes incorrigible, ugliness becomes inhuman, and uselessness becomes untrainable."[3] Accordingly, it is the status of chronicity, not that of disability, that has determined the fate of generations of people.

THE "NO-CODE" ORDER

As I learned more about John Lovelace and his life story, I came to question whether the designation of mental retardation had ever resulted in better care and treatment for him. On the contrary, as his history unfolded it seemed to me that he had most often been the subject of control rather than care, and that he had lived within a system designed to protect society from the perceived chronicity of his "uselessness." The moments of care that would become evident were individual acts of kindness. The system designed in the name of caring for people described as being mentally retarded emerged clearly, and on the contrary, as a mechanism for the protection of others.

On May 29, 1987, the attorney with the Virginia Department for Rights of the Disabled who was assisting me in my inquiry concerning the "no-code" order for John contacted the physician who had written it. In her letter to him she explained my concern over whether John really had the ability to understand the full meaning of the decision and whether he was genuinely capable of giving informed consent for the order. She worded her letter in keeping with my assumption that John had never been declared incompetent and, therefore, may not have been helped with the decision by a guardian or advocate. After presenting my concerns to the physician, she asked that he explain the circumstances surrounding the decision and the nature of John's health problems. She also asked that he send copies of John's medical records for the last two years. She enclosed a copy of the release form that John had signed for me a few weeks earlier granting us access to his records.

Just over a month later the attorney wrote saying that she had not received a reply from the physician or the Burrell Home. She also informed me that she had resigned her position and that my case would be reassigned in a few weeks. I was disappointed that she was leaving, as she seemed sincerely interested and very competent. In fact, through my experience in attempting to secure information about what was happening in John Lovelace's life I came to believe that it must be very difficult for legal assistance programs like the Virginia Department for Rights of the Disabled to recruit and maintain lawyers of her quality. I suspect that the resources are simply not available to these agencies to adequately meet the needs of those who call on them for help. I say this because, even though the agency seemed to be doing its best to address my concern, it took three attorneys and over a year's time before my questions about John would be answered.

The attorney to whom my questions were reassigned seemed suspicious of my motives for getting involved in John Lovelace's life. He questioned the appropriateness of my concern about John's ability to make a life-and-death decision when the battle for self-determination which had been waged in recent years by, as he said, "advocates like yourself" was, in fact, for the right of disabled people to make more of their own decisions. As I later learned, he had actually received some of the information requested from the physician by the end of July. In response to my telephone inquiry to him at that time, however, he answered that he was still investigating and would not be able to discuss any findings with me anyway until I had obtained additional release forms with the signatures of John and two witnesses. I secured these releases, sent them to him, and waited to hear something. No word came. I wrote again in September asking to be advised on the progress of the case. I received no reply. I wrote in October, and again in November. In January 1988 I was informed that this lawyer had left the agency and that my case had been assigned to yet another attorney.

John Gifford, my third attorney, pursued the matter aggressively and capably. He kept me informed of his actions and the results. He has my thanks and respect. On January 19 he sent a copy of the physician's letter and attached Burrell Home material that had been received by his predecessor in July. The letter from John's physician gave an explanation of the case and his actions. He said that in response to John having severe headaches a CT scan of his head had been ordered. The examination revealed an infarction, an area of dead tissue, in the brain. A neurosurgeon was then consulted who declared that John's condition did not make him a candidate for surgery. The letter continued:

> In March of 1987, Mr. Lovelace became more lethargic and I became more concerned about our course of action if he were to sustain a cardiac

or respiratory arrest. I then attempted to locate any relatives or next of kin to discuss this situation. However, I was informed that there was no record of any next of kin and that Mr. Lovelace was handling his affairs . . . I discussed with Mr. Lovelace his medical condition, the CT scan report, and . . . [the neurosurgeon's report]. I then asked his desires in the event of cardiac or pulmonary arrest and the maintenance of life systems following such. Mr. Lovelace indicated to me that he did not want resuscitative measures in case of cardiopulmonary arrest. I concurred and indicated on 3-24-87, to the . . . [adult home], his "no code" status . . . If questions remain regarding Mr. Lovelace and these steps, please communicate with me.

My immediate response as I read the physician's final comment was a mixture of anger and confusion. How could it be that this letter had been sitting on a lawyer's desk or in his files for six months and I had not even been given the courtesy of being informed how the inquiry was progressing? More importantly, how could it be that what appeared to me to be a glaring inconsistency had not been questioned? The no-code order was written on March 24, 1987, in part founded on the stated fact that John had no next of kin. The documentation for the order that had been included with his letter, however, was dated March 25, 1987. It reads as follows:

Per your request, this is confirmation that we have no record of John Lovelace having any next of kin. I have also taken the liberty to see if Mental Health Services had any such records and they also have no record of any next of kin.

In writing this letter the social worker had gone beyond what had been requested of her; she had checked with at least one source outside of the Burrell Home for possible information on relatives. Still, the search was certainly not vigorous. Most striking, however, is the unmistakable fact that the order was issued the day *before* there was any documentation that there were no next of kin on record.

Before I contacted John Gifford about this issue, however, I received a call from him with even more startling news. John Lovelace was no longer living in the Burrell Home in Roanoke. There had been concerns at Burrell about his increasing behavioral problems, and he had been transferred temporarily to a psychiatric rehabilitation center. There it was determined that placement in the Burrell Home was no longer appropriate for him and he had been discharged. He had then been moved to a small adult home in a rural area just outside of Roanoke. The dynamics of the move still remain a puzzle to me. I still don't know whether John was discharged because of a real worsening in his behavior or whether my "meddling" caused him to be perceived as a problem to be gotten rid of.

John Gifford continued to pursue the matter, and his inquiries continued to uncover more surprises. On April 4 he received a letter from the social worker at the Burrell Home with a page from John's medical record. It revealed a troubling new revelation. John's no code order had been changed the previous September! In the letter she said:

> Enclosed you will find the Doctors Order Sheet for the month of September in 1987. This is the copy of the orders that . . . [the doctor] wrote to rescind the No Code order on John Lovelace.
>
> The attached Order Sheet contained the following comments:
>
> Previous order for NO CODE is rescinded. Pt. is a full code. All heroic measures should be attempted in the [case of] cardiac or pulmonary arrest.

John Gifford wrote again to the physician, this time concerning the change in John's no-code order. On May 5th he received a response:

> This letter serves to clear up any confusion that may exist over the wishes of John Lovelace regarding heroic resuscitative measures.
>
> Mr. Lovelace was a patient of mine several years ago, who initially decided that in the event of massive brain hemorrhage or other medical catastrophe, he did not desire heroic resuscitative measures.
>
> Because there was some confusion regarding this documentation on his . . . chart, he was re-approached by me and in the presence of the . . . Burrell Home for Adults Nursing Supervisor . . . he then decided that *he did* want resuscitative measures.
>
> This was duly noted and documented in his chart. Subsequent to this, Mr. Lovelace left the . . . Burrell Home for Adults and my care.
>
> To my knowledge . . . [at] this time, his desire for heroic resuscitative measures remains in force.

The physician who wrote this letter was part of a system that was designed and functioned for purposes other than the care for people like John Lovelace. I have not revealed the physician's name because to focus on his individual actions, motives, and values would misdirect attention from the significance of the life of John Lovelace and his encounters with a culture that consistently viewed him as a problem to be managed and controlled. For the same reason there are other names that I have deleted from John's story.

It was important, however, that I shared with you the name of John Gifford. He was active, concerned, and persistent in finding the details of what had happened in the case of John Lovelace up to that time. I wrote to him on May 23, 1988:

Thanks so much for your recent letter and the copy of . . . [the doctor's letter] to you. I was fascinated by the manner in which he explained his change in John's chart concerning resuscitative measures. It seems incredible that he has not addressed at all the question of John's ability to make an informed decision for a 'no-code' order. I am more convinced than ever, however, that our actions on this issue have made a real difference in John's best interests. I also believe that other mentally retarded persons may ultimately benefit from our advocacy in John's case.

I also appreciate the copy of your letter to Bob Williams [the owner of the small adult home where John was now living]. I am glad we will have formal documentation that John's current physician has not placed any restrictions on emergency medical treatment in his case.

I visited John at Little Ponderosa [his new home] two weeks ago. I think that the living conditions are a significant improvement for John over what he had at the Burrell Home. The size (17 men), the country atmosphere, and the apparently positive relationships among people there makes it appear to be a much more positive environment for him. I talked with Bob Williams for a while and came away feeling that he has a genuine and personal concern for the residents of his facility.

As always, I appreciate the energy and commitment you are giving to the concern we share for John Lovelace and the larger implications of his case. I will be calling soon just to chat about some other information I have found on John's background. Take care.

In early June John Gifford wrote saying that he was pleased that things seemed to be better for John Lovelace in his new home. Most importantly, however, he said that he was leaving the Department for Rights of the Disabled effective the same day. He expressed best wishes for John and said he was glad to have been able to work on his behalf. I never met John Gifford, but on John Lovelace's behalf I continue to thank him.

CHAPTER 5

Becoming Invisible

BEING VISIBLE: A MOTHER'S LOVE

When the writer Ralph Ellison died in 1994, a flood of media attention was focused on his novel, *Invisible Man*. First published in 1952, it was not, as the title suggests, a work of science fiction. Instead, it is an autobiographical account of the life of a young African American man. Through his narrative he relates his experiences of social and personal isolation in segregated and racist America. In the opening paragraph, Ellison's character declares:

> I am an invisible man. No, I am not a spook like those who haunted Edgar Allen Poe; nor am I one of your Hollywood movie ectoplasms. I am a man of substance, of flesh and bone, fiber and liquids—I might even be said to possess a mind. I am invisible, understand, simply because people refuse to see me.[1]

Ellison's character goes on to explain that his invisibility is created because others view him with eyes that are dominated by prejudice, bias, and false assumptions.

> That invisibility to which I refer occurs because of a peculiar disposition of the eyes of those with whom I come in contact. A matter of the construction of their inner eyes ... you often doubt if you really exist. You wonder whether you aren't simply a phantom in other people's minds.[2]

Ellison's powerful words about the construction by "inner eyes" helped his readers understand in a new way the experience of race as more than a set of physical characteristics or a shared social history.

Ellison demonstrated that the meaning of ethnic differences has often been constructed by powerful majority groups in ways that have resulted in the oppression of vulnerable people. There has also been a long history of the social construction of the meaning of disability. These constructions have created the invisibility of people with disabilities analogous to the invisibility created by racism. It is also important to understand that people with different disabilities may experience different degrees of invisibility. People with intellectual disabilities have been among the most socially invisible of all people with disabilities. The life of John Lovelace is a testament to this tragic fact.

John Lovelace was loved and nurtured by his foster mother. She understood his differences and embraced him as an individual of worth from his infancy into adolescence. Her love made him visible as a person. She also believed that she was doing what was best for him when she committed him to the institution in Lynchburg. She could not have known, of course, that her loving act was the beginning of his journey into invisibility.

The medical notes for Patient 6839 at the Virginia State Colony begin on the day he was admitted, October 14, 1948. John Lovelace at age 18 was found to be in fair physical condition. He was accompanied by his mother and was described as looking like a "simple feebleminded individual." Over the next few days he was given several laboratory tests and he was X-rayed. No health problems were found. He was placed first on Ward 19, was then moved to Ward 4, and then to Ward 10. The moves seemed to have been part of the normal process of finding the most appropriate living area for patients.

On November 16, just over a month after his admission to the institution, John went home to Martinsville on a 10-day pass. The notes indicate that seven days later his pass was converted to a parole in the care of his foster mother until January 1, 1949. In December his parole was extended until February 1. The note for February 1 reads:

> Mother of patient returned him to the Colony today and reported to Dr. Harrell [the superintendent] that John had a job in a sawmill and [was] getting along fine. She asked for an extension of the furlough and this was granted through March 1, 1949.

This furlough was again extended until March 31, when Mrs. Hunter returned John to the Colony. The notes for that day indicate that it was her hope that she would soon take him back to Martinsville again.

> Letter request for return of parole . . . produced by Mrs. W. . . . I. Hunter, Martinsville, Virginia, custodian of above named patient. Patient pleasant, immature, clean, neat, tidy, in excellent state of health, free from evidence of infectious disease or somatic malady. Patient has been working, $.70 per hour, weather permitting with Messrs. Morris Doyle Lumber Company, total wages $58.40. Camp [the lumbar camp] removed to other area. Now hopes to be a "fixer" in local textile mill. Mrs. Hunter reports excellent community adjustment, patient for reevaluation, and recheck dental, physical, X-ray and psychology; and hopes for recommendation of indoor mill employment under direction. Patient readily and cheerfully goes to Hospital Ward.

Two weeks later, John was again paroled to the care of his foster mother. At this point he had been on the rolls of the institution for seven months but had been in residence for only six weeks. Letters Mrs. Hunter wrote to the Colony help explain why John was only partially institutionalized. They are printed here as they were written. The grammar and spelling must be understood as expressions from a poor woman with limited education but, as will be evident, a wealth of compassion.

1-22 1948

D. L. Harrell Jr. M.D.
Dear sir
  in Regards to my son John R. Lovelace that I have at home on a ten day visit he seems very well and so Happy to be at home that I am asking if you will Extend his visit for some time and if he does not get a long all Right I will Braing back there. I will be Responsible for him untill you think it best to braing him back there.
Yours very truly

Mrs. Hunter wrote several other times requesting the parole extensions that John was granted. One letter, written after she had returned him to the Colony for examinations and evaluations is particularly revealing of her concern for her son.

4-12 1948

D. L. Harrell Jr. M.D.
Dear sir
  I did Return John R. Lovelace to the Colony on March 31 not that I found it necessary to do so as his conduct was about perfect while he was here but you wanted him for further treatment of some kind have you completed your study of him and can you give me a certificate so

he can work he has a chance now to learn a trade which is much higher work than he has been doing and much better pay and lots safer it is under union and he can not work there unless I can get sertificate from you stating he is capable of working unless we can Hurry things up a bit I am afraid he will loose this chance at learning a trade so please see what you can do and let me [know] real soon.

Yours very truly

John returned to the Colony briefly in July 1949; he was sterilized at that time. The medical staff at the institution recommended this, of course, and Mrs. Hunter agreed that it was a good idea. As discussed earlier, at the time it would have been viewed as serving society's best interests and, it would have been argued, it was for John's benefit as well.

John was discharged from the Lynchburg facility in March 1951. He had officially been a patient at the institution for almost two and a half years. In fact, he had been in residence there for less than two months during that period. Most of the time he had been in Martinsville with the person who seems to have cared more for him than anyone else did or ever would, Mrs. Hunter. In February prior to John's discharge, she responded to a social worker who had written to her saying that it was customary to discharge a patient who had been on parole as long as John, and asking how he had been doing at home. Mrs. Hunter was obviously ready for John's ties to the institution to be dissolved completely. She was hopeful for her adopted son's future.

February 20, 1951
Martinsville, Va.

...I do not see any reason why my son John R. Lovelace should not be discharge from the Institution as he has not given any trouble in any way since he has been home and has been working with the Lester Hardwood Flooring Co. for the past 9 months and he works with sirule Hundred men and gets on with them all right as far as I know he makes ninty cts a hour and will get a bonus twice a year after working his first 6 months and most of the time he works nine hours a day and is unusual good about going on his job and as far as I can see he is living a very normal Life No drinking no smoking attends church regular and dose not seem to care much for women that is I very seldom even see him with one So I think he can make it all right now and thank you very much for your kindness in writing to me.

Yours very truly

The social worker must have followed up on this letter with a visit or telephone call. In a letter she wrote to the Department of Public

Welfare in Martinsville about John's upcoming discharge the social worker described in more detail his positive life in the community.

I talked with Mr. and Mrs. Hunter, Foster Parents, of the above named man. They seemed to be very pleased with John's adjustment. It seems that he has a job with Lester Lumbar Company and is doing well in this work. He does not make friends easily, but he and his father are getting along much better and they attend movies and church together. These two activities are the boy's main social outlets. He pays his mother so much a week toward his room and board. Mrs. Hunter stated that it was the boy's desire to do this and she thought that maybe it was a good thing since it gave him the feeling of standing on his feet. He has remained well physically since he has returned, with the exception of an appendix operation, he has had no illnesses. Mrs. Hunter also stated that he was much calmer and was not subject to fits of anger as he was before.

They are real pleased with his being home and hope that they will be able to keep him.

John's foster mother's full name was Zenia Leslie Hunter. I am convinced that she deeply loved her foster son. Her letters reflect a genuine and persevering concern for him. John knew that he had been born to another woman, but he also knew that it was Mrs. Hunter who was the source of his nurturance.

When I first talked with John about his background, what he said about his mother confused me. His speech was very difficult to understand and I was not sure how much of my confusion was due to misunderstanding what he was saying, and how much of it might be due to a problem with John's memory of his childhood. He spoke of his mother being dead, and on one occasion he told me that she was "killed by a boy." At another time he told me his mother had been killed by a car. Months later the confusion was cleared up after I did some digging into courthouse records and newspaper files in Martinsville.

Etta Lovelace, John's mother at his birth, was indeed "killed by a boy." In 1936, when John was six years old and living with the Hunters, Etta Lovelace was working as a domestic helper in a home near Martinsville. One morning as she was churning butter in the kitchen, the fifteen-year-old son of the family passed through carrying a rifle on his way to go outside. His rifle accidently fired and Etta was killed. *The Daily Bulletin* of Martinsville described the accident this way:

Sheriff J. . . . M. Davis and Coroner J. . . . W. Simmons, called to the scene of the shooting for an inquest, learned that young Turner had picked up the gun, a 22 calibre rifle, in a bedroom of the home to go outside and do a little target shooting. As he passed through the kitchen and started out the door, he attempted to unbreech the weapon, and as he did so, it accidentally went off, the discharge striking the woman who was nearby churning, the bullet entering the right side of the abdomen. The woman died within a minute after being wounded. A sister of the youth, Virginia Turner, was washing dishes and barely missed being in the range of the bullet.

Young Turner said he was unaware that the gun was loaded, that he was in the act of unbreeching it when it accidentally went off.

Etta was described in the article as being the daughter of the late John Lovelace, whose obituary, in fact, appeared in *The Daily Bulletin* on April 1, 1932. One of the first bits of information that I shared with John as
I attempted to recapture some of his personal history was that he was very likely named for his maternal grandfather. He was pleased with this idea.

Two days after her death *The Daily Bulletin* reported that the Turner boy had been cleared of any charges in the killing. Technical charges of manslaughter were dropped after the case was heard in the county court. The article also mentioned that Etta had been living with the Turner family ever since the death of her father.

John was so young when his mother died and his contact with her so limited that his memories of her were naturally vague. He was not able to tell me whether he saw her often. He simply remembered that she had "long hair and she was pretty." It is likely that Mrs. Hunter instilled in him the memory that Etta was killed by a boy with a gun. Whatever the case, that was all that he had to remember her by. Her death did not seem to be a traumatic recollection for him.

In contrast, the only time I saw John weep openly was when he told me that his mother had been killed by a car. As I sorted out my confusion concerning the two stories of the gun and the car, I came to understand why he was so moved by the latter story. The woman who was killed by an automobile was John's *real* mother, his nurturer, protector and encourager: Mrs. Hunter.

INVISIBILITY BEGINS

Three years after John was discharged from the institution at the request of his foster mother, she was killed on a highway outside of Martinsville. Apparently things had been going well in John's life. There were no reports to the contrary. Then he lost the most important person in his life, the one person who cared deeply about him. *The Bulletin* report said:

Mrs. Zenia Leslie Hunter, 59-year-old North Martinsville resident, was killed early Tuesday night when struck by an automobile ... The accident occurred on route 890 near Snow Creek, in Franklin County, 15 miles north of Martinsville ... Mrs. Hunter was believed to have been waiting by the roadside for the Rocky Mount-Martinsville bus when she saw a motor vehicle approaching from the north. In attempting to cross from the eastside to the westside of the highway, she was struck ... in the center of the southbound lane of the highway ... Mrs. Hunter died en route to the Martinsville General Hospital. Death resulted from head and internal injuries ... Mrs. Hunter, born in Greyson County in 1895, had made her home here for the past 27 years. She was a member of the Church of Jesus Christ of Latter Day Saints.

Surviving are her husband, William I. Hunter; one daughter ... a foster son, John Lovelace, and three grandchildren ...

When Mrs. Hunter died on the highway that evening much of the hope and potential in John Lovelace's life died with her. His mother, his advocate, the one who most clearly saw him as a human being, was gone.

CHAPTER 6

Broken Ties
"Addressee Unknown"

"MINIMALLY GIFTED"

While studying as a doctoral candidate at Columbia University, I was blessed with having professors who were wonderful scholars. They were also people of impressive character and deep compassion. One of my mentors was Ignacy Goldberg. As all outstanding teachers do, he often shared stories from his own life with his students. One of his stories that I have frequently recalled, and perhaps altered or embellished in some ways, is of his experiences while working in an institution for people with intellectual disabilities in Indiana.

Professor Goldberg remembered that during his first days at the institution, an experienced staff member explained to him that there were actually three populations of residents living there. He described the three groups as the "retarded retarded," the "normal retarded," and the "minimally gifted." According to this classification, the retarded retarded were those people who needed constant care and attention. They could not survive without the help that was given to them by other people (often including help from the normal retarded and the minimally gifted). The normal retarded were those people who constituted the mainstream population of the institution. They cared for themselves for the most part and functioned in a relatively independent fashion within the institutional culture. They were often given the most basic and unpleasant chores to do by the staff. Their work was often supervised by the minimally gifted, who made sure that things ran smoothly in the wards of the institution, and who occupied the upper echelon of the residential population. The minimally gifted were commonly rewarded by the institution's staff for doing the things the staff was actually being paid to do. Their rewards varied from cigarettes, to special privileges, to money, and other favors.

The quality of life and the standard of care for many of the other residents frequently depended on the abilities, sensibilities, and compassion of the minimally gifted. Dr. Goldberg discussed the degrading nature of the words used to describe the residents, particularly the sarcasm of the designation "minimally gifted." The observations behind the descriptions, however, he found to be valid. There were distinctly different populations of people in the institutions designed and operated for *the* retarded, a supposedly monolithic group.

I have often thought of Dr. Goldberg's story while visiting residential facilities for people identified as being mentally retarded. I believe I have seen the scenario of the three castes of retarded people in those institutions played out a number of times. Recalling his portrayal of the hierarchies and population differences in institutions helped me understand some of the social dynamics and individual behavior that I have observed.

LISTENING TO TOM

A striking confirmation of Dr. Goldberg's recollection came to me recently when I stumbled onto a short story by Jack London entitled *Told in the Drooling Ward.* It was written from the perspective of a resident in a state mental retardation institution in the early twentieth century. London admired the work of the eugenicists, and his philosophy included the assumption that many of the mental and physical limitations found in individuals had racial and social-class origins. London's character in the story, Tom, repeats several times that the institution is the right place for him to be, and he implies that the outside world is too complex and competitive for his ability to cope. On the other hand, London has Tom explain the ways in which he is superior to others within his institutional world and how they rely on his abilities for their well-being. Tom's description of the differences among the people in the institution make the story a compelling reading experience for anyone interested in the sociology of institutionalization.

> Me? I'm not a drooler. I'm the assistant. I don't know what Miss Jones or Miss Kelsey could do without me. There are fifty-five low-grade droolers in this ward, and how could they ever all be fed if I wasn't around? I like

to feed the droolers. They don't make much trouble. They can't. Something's wrong with most of their legs and arms and they can't talk. They are very low-grade. I can walk, and talk, and do things. You must be careful with the droolers and not feed them too fast . . . Miss Jones says I'm an expert. When a new nurse comes I show her how to do it. It's funny watching a new nurse try to feed them. She goes at it so slow and careful that suppertime would be around before she finished shoving down their breakfast. Then I show her, because I'm an expert. Dr. Dalrymple says I am, and he ought to know . . . [1]

Tom goes into further detail about his special place in the hierarchy of the institution. He also divulges the fact that there are people in the institution who have been placed there because of epilepsy and that he doesn't like them. He clearly thinks that they don't belong in what he calls the Home.

But I am a high-grade feeb. Dr. Dalrymple says I am too smart to be in the Home, but I never let on. It's a pretty good place. And I don't throw fits like lots of the feebs. You see that house up there through the trees. The high-grade epilecs all live in it by themselves. They're stuck up because they ain't ordinary feebs. They call it the clubhouse, and they say they're just as good as anyone outside, only they're sick. I don't like them much. They laugh at me, when they ain't busy throwing fits. But I don't care . . . Low-grade epilecs are disgusting and high-grade epilecs put on airs.

I'm glad I ain't an epilec. There ain't anything to them. They just talk big, that's all.[2]

Tom also describes several of his fellow residents according to the etiology of their retardation. His description of the characteristics and prognosis associated with each diagnosis is interesting and, in some cases, moving.

Do you know what a micro is? It's the kind with the little heads no bigger than your fist. They're usually droolers, and they live a long time. The hydros don't drool. They have the big heads, and they're smarter. But they never grow up. They always die. I never look at one without thinking he's going to die. Sometimes, when I'm feeling lazy, or the nurse is mad at me, I wish I was a drooler with nothing to do and someone to feed me. But I guess I'd sooner talk and be what I am.[3]

JOHN: BACK FOR THE LONG HAUL

In the early afternoon of September 9, 1957, John Lovelace was again admitted to what was by then known as the Lynchburg Training

School and Hospital. He was not a "drooler." He would soon be taking care of other people in the institution.

He was given a new patient number, #8998. The admission form indicated that he had been living in a rooming house in Martinsville prior to his admission. He was delivered to the institution by Mrs. Hunter's daughter. On the admission questionnaire she indicated that she was not related to John. On another form she did indicate, however, that she was a friend. John was, in fact, admitted on a petition by Mrs. Hunter's daughter. She said that he could not care for himself and that he had no living relatives.

In the report of the physical examination he was given upon admission, the examining physician noted that although syphilis had been mentioned in the past as a possible reason for John's disabilities, he was "completely without the stigmata of congenital syphilis." During my research on John's life I noticed in earlier records that there were notations of negative tests for syphilis for John. The same was true for Etta Lovelace when she was institutionalized for the purpose of sterilization. The physician further noted that the "general picture is of natal trauma," and he thought that John's disabilities had been caused by birth injuries. He diagnosed John as having cerebral palsy and associated mental retardation. This is consistent with what I know of and observed about John. I believe that the "drawing spells" he was reported to have had as an infant were likely seizures. John had seizures most of his life, not an uncommon accompaniment to cerebral palsy and mental retardation. His seizures were fairly well controlled with medication in the later years of his adult life, and no seizures were noted during the period when I knew him.

After mental testing, a psychologist found that John showed "decided improvement in the test results compared with those of previous commitment." The comment was made that he had apparently learned to make maximum use of his capacity and "could probably continue to assist in his own care as he did in the past but since there is no one to give him any good supervision, he will probably need to remain here." This was a sad observation, but one that proved to be very true. The first time he was committed he spent only a few weeks actually in residence in the institution. The rest of the time he was on parole with Mrs. Hunter. This time John would spend 22 years in the Lynchburg Training School and Hospital, with only a few days lived outside its gates. He was 27 when he was committed. He would be 49 before he left. During those 22 years he would become completely lost to the world he had known before. All his ties of relationship and friendship would be lost. At the end of those 22 years he would find himself completely alone in the world.

Early in his stay in the institution a psychologist noticed that John was sensitive about his speech. She said that he apparently tried to conceal his speech impairment by talking in a voice too low to be heard.

> When he speaks in a usual tone, he is able to communicate rather well. When asked to repeat, he not only becomes upset and lowers his voice but actually seems to get confused on what he is trying to say. These characteristics, of course, interfere with demonstration of his actual functioning level.

Communication continued to be a problem throughout his life. It was difficult to understand John even after I had become accustomed to his speech pattern. It was very frustrating to him when he was not understood, even after repeated attempts. I often wondered just what John could tell me in depth about his life if only I could have understood him better.

During the Christmas holidays of the first two years that John was in the institution he went home to Martinsville. The records indicate that he spent at least a week each of those two years sharing the holiday with Mrs. Hunter's daughter and her family. The third year he did not go home for Christmas. He received a package. Mrs. Hunter's daughter had written earlier to John's social worker asking for his clothing sizes.

In November 1961, John's social worker sent a letter to Mrs. Hunter's daughter suggesting a Christmas visit for John.

> It has been several years since John Lovelace has had a vacation away from the institution, and he has asked if it might be possible for you to have him for a short visit during the Christmas holidays this year. It would mean a great deal to John to be able to be in a home for a few days, and we would appreciate very much your taking him. If it is not convenient for you to have him over Christmas Day, perhaps we can arrange a New Year's visit. John has money and could pay his own transportation by bus.
>
> We are enclosing a vacation form and a list of furlough instructions to help you in planning a trip for John, and we look forward to hearing from you.

As a result of the letter, John went home on a bus and stayed for a week.

The next year a similar letter was sent with the superintendent's signature. This time there was a different response.

Dear Mr. Nagler,

It is impossible at this time for me to have John home. The way that I am working there would be no one home all day and John would be by himself. I think Christmas would mean more to him there with the nice Christmas program you have set up.

Maybe we can have him home during the spring vacation. I will be on vacation and be at home with him.

I am very sorry that I have to say no at this time.

Letters continued to go out for several years around the holidays suggesting a visit home for John. However, there was never another response. A final attempt to contact the family was made in January 1978.

We are writing to bring you up to date on Mr. Lovelace's progress. He was recently transferred from living unit 2D to 3D within the Social Skills Center. He was promoted as a result of his continued good behavior. We feel that he is making progress. He seems to understand why he must learn to deal with anger in a more constructive manner than acting out at others. We hope he will continue to work with us.

Family contact can be used to encourage appropriate behavior. We urge you and other interested individuals to visit and correspond frequently. You are invited to meet with us to discuss the programs Mr. Lovelace is enrolled in. We hope to hear from you soon.

The letter was returned marked "Addressee Unknown." John's last tie to family and community had been severed.

BROKEN BONDS

My portrayal of the breaking of bonds between his family and John is not meant to be a condemnation of them. Rather, it is offered as an example of a systemic tendency. Institutions for people with mental retardation, like other residential institutions, have functioned to separate and isolate their residents, even from their own families. The term "colony" was very appropriate for such institutions. People were colonized within these institutions away from the "home country" of their culture. They tended to be forgotten by the society from which they were removed. The longer they remained colonized, the greater the risk that the ties to family and community would be weakened. If they stayed long enough, the chances were great that the ties would be severed completely.

There is a very good reason why most mental retardation institutions have their own graveyards. People who lived in these institutions for most of their lives were at high risk of outliving their connections to the external world. When they died there was no one to claim them, no one from the outside world to grieve for them. They did not escape the colony even in death. Some families maintained interest and contact and continued to care, but maintaining ties across institutional walls is extremely hard work. It takes a very strong family, or friend, or community to withstand the wearing away of the bonds of relationship by separation and isolation. It is no accident that most of the large mental retardation institutions were built in out-of-the-way places. The facilities were not intended to be a *part* of society. They were intended to be *apart* from society. The same was as true of the occupants as of those buildings.

The letter making reference to the importance of John's learning to control his anger defines a long-standing problem for him. It continued to be so for most of his life. It was anger that first prompted Mrs. Hunter to have him institutionalized. The shock of that separation from her may have been one of the reasons for his dramatic and positive change, and his quick parole and discharge. I suspect that after her death he engaged in angry outbursts, which may have led to his second commitment into the institution. I think I can understand his anger. I imagine that if I had grown up with the physical, social, and psychological cuts and bruises that he lived with I might be even angrier. When I came to know him, I saw him at times react with anger when he did not know what else to do— when he was frustrated, frightened, or hurting. Anger is a basic and strong emotion, one readily available to us. He used it, I am convinced, as a way of trying to survive. Unfortunately, he used it at great cost. He was usually the one who suffered the most from his angry outbursts.

During his long stay in the Lynchburg Training School and Hospital from 1957 to 1979, John was involved in more than 30 serious fights. This number may only be the tip of the iceberg. These are the fights that were serious enough to be recorded in his patient records. Loosened teeth, abrasions, lacerations, and stitches were commonplace in his life. Although he often took the first swing, it seems he usually was on the losing side of his battles. His poor balance and lack of coordination did not serve him well in these confrontations. He was also punished for his involvement in these altercations. For example, on June 3, 1960, his record shows: "John got into a fight with Harvey B. Discipline: Lock up on ward 22C, for three days."

LEARNING TO SURVIVE

John's records consistently showed that he liked to work. That proved true in my own experience with him. He liked to be busy and useful. He liked to earn money. Having a little pocket money seemed to be important to him as one of the few available symbols of independence in his life. To have the opportunity to work has often been an earned privilege in institutions of varied kinds. Whether it be the inmate, patient, or institutionalized person by some other name, it is considered an elevation in status to be trusted to work.

In some cases the work done by patients in institutions was not officially sanctioned or recognized. The more able patients, as observed by Dr. Goldberg and Jack London, often did work that was assigned to the paid staff. In return they received cigarettes, privileges, praise, and tips. In other cases there were formal work programs that provided patients with rewards or minimal monetary return for their efforts. In 1959 John was described in his patient notes as a "working patient, helps to take care of patients." This was obviously an officially recognized program.

His angry outbursts sometimes were incompatible with his working role. A note in 1965 said: "During the daytime he does good work, according to the attendant, but occasionally has to be reprimanded because he has a rather explosive temper." Several times during the decade of the 1960s he was referred to as a "working boy" in the notes. "Boy," a curious term for a man in his late thirties, recalls the way that the term was used offensively to refer to mature African American men. It was common in institutions for "working patients" to do much of the dressing, bathing, and toileting of the less able patients. This reality is reflected in an entry in John's medical file in 1968. "Patient slipped when coming out of the doorway of the tub room with [another] patient in his arms. FINDINGS: Contusion of the right hip."

During the early 1970s work programs that were intended to provide training and skill development that could eventually be used outside the institution became common. This was part of the growing movement toward the de-institutionalization of patients who could be prepared to live in the community. John was involved in what was called the Work Activity Center. Again, tension apparently existed between his ability to do good work and his behavior problems. In March of 1973 the notes say, "The Work Activity Center has reported that Mr. Lovelace has been suspended from this placement several times because of his abusive behavior . . . It is reported, however, that Mr. Lovelace is a good worker and has been given added responsibilities because of this." John eventually proved himself competent through this program and was employed by the Sheltered Workshop in Lynchburg. He later worked during summers at the Jefferson Car Wash in Lynchburg and did yard work for a local physician.

JUST LIKE ALL OTHER MEN

In the latter half of the decade of the 1970s the de-institutionalization movement reached its peak. The idea that people with disabilities should live in communities rather than in institutions was embraced in both professional and political circles. People were moved out of institutions in large numbers. John Lovelace was one of them.

On May 29, 1979, John was placed on leave in Kennedy House, an adult home in Martinsville. He also went to work at a sheltered workshop there. Plans began to be formulated that after he completed training at the workshop he would be placed in a job elsewhere in Martinsville. After a few months he was described as having made a very good adjustment to his new job and home. Professionals at the Lynchburg Training School and Hospital, and at Kennedy House, agreed that the time had come for John to be discharged from the institution.

On November 20, 1979, John received a letter signed by his social worker and the director of the Lynchburg Training School and Hospital.

> Dear John:
>
> I am writing to let you know that your discharge is final on November 21, 1979.
>
> If you remember from my last visit with you, this will mean that you are now completely free from Lynchburg Training School and Hospital. You can live and work in Martinsville, forever, just like all other men in our country.
>
> Please remember to try and save your money, and to listen to what Ms. Robertson, the nurses, the aides, and Mr. Poole tell you. They care a lot about you and want to help you do what is best. Also, you must remember to control your temper and not get in any fights.
>
> All of us here at the Lynchburg Training School and Hospital are very, very proud of how well you are doing in Martinsville. We are very happy to be able to give you your discharge. I have enjoyed working with you, and will come to visit you again when I am in Martinsville.

CHAPTER 7

Looking Backward, Looking Forward

LOOKING BACKWARD

Edward Bellamy, social critic and philosopher, journalist and novelist, was a strident voice for societal reform during the late 1800s. His most influential work was entitled *Looking Backward*. This book, originally published in 1888, was a popular bestseller for years following its release. It was also very influential among American intellectuals at the time. In 1935, the philosopher and educator John Dewey ranked *Looking Backward* as one of the most important books published in the preceding 50 years.

Bellamy's novel is the story of Julian West, a man who falls into a trancelike sleep in 1887 and emerges from his coma in the year 2000. West awakens to a United States that has abandoned war, abolished political parties, and obliterated poverty. Every person is an equal shareholder in the responsibilities and benefits of citizenship, and all have equitable and sufficient incomes. Throughout the book Julian West finds that in the year 2000 American society is deeply committed to the equality of all of its citizens.

West's guide and interpreter of the new millennium world into which he has awakened is a physician named Dr. Leete. One of Leete's most profound revelations to Julian is that people with disabilities are considered to be equal members of his society. When West expresses surprise that what he refers to as charity has become so prevalent in the United States of 2000, an intriguing exchange takes place between the two men.

> Charity! Repeated Dr. Leete. Did you suppose that we consider the incapable class we are talking of objects of charity? Why naturally, I said inasmuch as they are incapable of self-support. But here the doctor took me up quickly. Who is capable of self-support? He demanded. There is no such thing in a civilized society as self-support ... from the moment that men begin to live together, and constitute even the rudest sort of society, self-support becomes impossible. As men grow more civilized ... a complex mutual dependence becomes the universal rule.[1]

Dr. Leete continues with an assertion of the fundamental equality of all people, regardless of individual needs or limitations, or in independence and productivity. Of this Julian questions, "How can they who produce nothing claim a share of the product as a right?" Dr. Leete answers that each generation in a society essentially inherits most of what it knows and possesses. He asks of West and his world of 1889:

> How did you come to be possessors of this knowledge and this machinery which represents nine parts to the one contributed by yourself in the value of your product? You inherited it, did you not? And were not these others, these unfortunate and crippled brothers whom you cast out, joint inheritors, co-heirs with you? What I do not understand is, setting aside all considerations of justice or brotherly feeling toward the crippled and defective, how the workers of your day could have had any heart for their work, knowing that their children, or grandchildren, if unfortunate, would be deprived of the comforts and even necessities of life?[2]

Remarkable developments in molecular biology and genetic engineering are now reported in the news media almost daily. These advances in scientific knowledge and medical technology will almost certainly change the course of human history. The eradication of what are considered diseases, disorders, and defects may become a reality before the end of our new century. A critical question in this pursuit, however, may be how human diversity is defined. Are disabilities, from this perspective, defects or human differences? Is disability a condition to be prevented in all circumstances or is it part of the spectrum of human variation? Depending upon the answer, what does this say about the status of people with disabilities in a democracy? What does it say about their fundamental equality as people?

LOOKING FORWARD?

The danger that people with disabilities will be further devalued as genetic intervention techniques become increasing available is illustrated by recent remarks made by James Watson. Winner of the Nobel Prize and codiscoverer of DNA, Watson was also the first director of the Human Genome Project. In his capacity as leader of the effort to map and sequence the genetic makeup of human beings, Watson also advocated careful consideration of the ethical, legal, and social implications of the Project. Yet in an article entitled *Looking Forward*, Watson dismissed the value of people with severe disabilities when he spoke of the decisions faced by "prospective parents when they learn that their prospective child carries a gene that would block its opportunity for a meaningful life."[3] In the same article, he speaks disapprovingly of parents who do not undergo genetic testing. "So we must also face up to the ethical and practical dilemma, facing these individuals who could have undergone genetic diagnosis, but who for one reason or another declined the opportunity and later gave birth to children who must face up to lives of hopeless inequality."[4]

More recently, Watson spoke to the German Congress of Molecular Medicine and condemned the eugenic philosophy that resulted in the atrocities of the Nazi era. Then, in an amazing contradiction, he advocated what might be termed *parental eugenics.* He asserted that the truly relevant question for most families is whether anything good could come from having a child with a major handicap. From this perspective, Watson said, "seeing the bright side of being handicapped is like praising the virtues of extreme poverty."[5] Watson's assertions stand in stark contrast to the questions he raised a few years earlier while he served as the director of the Human Genome Project:

> The question now faces us, as we work out the details of the human genetic message, as to how we are going to deal with these differences between individuals. In the past, at the time of the Eugenics movement in the United States and in England, and during the reign of racist thoughts in Nazi Germany, there was very little genetic knowledge. Most decisions then were made without solid genetic evidence. There were many prejudices, but almost no real human genetics. Now we have to face the fact that we soon will have real facts, and how are we going to respond to them? Who is going to take care of those people who are disabled by the genes they have inherited? How can we compensate them for the fact that many individuals are not as equal genetically as other people? I don't think we know the answers, and that is why we are here for this meeting.[6]

An even greater contrast to this statement is evident in his remarks concerning people with developmental disabilities and the possibility of a new eugenics movement.

> ... we must not fall into the trap of being against everything Hitler was for. It was in no way evil for Hitler to regard mental disease as a scourge on society ... because of Hitler's use of the term Master Race, we should not feel the need to say that we never want to use genetics to make humans more capable than they are today ... common sense tells us that if scientists find ways to greatly improve human capabilities, there will be no stopping the public from happily seizing them.[7]

Watson has advocated eugenic measures to prevent even mild disabilities, and he argues that most learning problems are genetic in origin.

> And what would be the consequences of isolating genes that give rise to the various forms of dyslexia, opening up the possibility that women will take antenatal tests to see if their prospective child is likely to have a bad reading disorder? Is it not conceivable that such tests would lead to our devoting less resources to the currently reading-handicapped children whom now we accept as an inevitable feature of human life?[8]
>
> If you are really stupid, I would call that a disease. The lower 10 percent who really have difficulty, even in elementary school, what's the cause of it? A lot of people would like to say, "Well, poverty, things like that." It probably isn't. So I'd get rid of that, to help the lower 10 percent.[9]

In *Backdoor to Eugenics,* Troy Duster argued that *eugenics* is alive and well in our society but in a more subtle manifestation. While it is still being presented as an economic and social issue, eugenics is also being presented as a matter of parental responsibility or irresponsibility. Although less overt, eugenics in its new form may be even more powerful than the earlier eugenics movement in its impact on the lives of people with disabilities.[10]

The eugenicists of the nineteenth and twentieth centuries looked to evolutionary theory and Mendelian genetics for moral guidelines. They believed that evolutionary theory and science could provide models for social ethics. The failure of this approach was evidenced in the needless institutionalization of people with disabilities who were deemed to be unfit for social struggle and in the needless sterilization of people inaccurately assessed to be the carriers of defective genes. Ultimately, the moral horrors of the Holocaust evolved from this philosophy.

"YOU ARE NOW COMPLETELY FREE"

In 1979 John Lovelace was discharged from the institution where he had been sequestered for more than 20 years. He was told that he was now a free and equal citizen of the United States of America. Soon, however, he would find himself in a country that continued to question whether there was anything of value in his life, whether he deserved a part of the social inheritance of his time.

"You are now completely free from Lynchburg Training School and Hospital," said the letter confirming John's discharge. "You can live and work in Martinsville, forever, just like all other men in our country." These encouraging and hopeful words, written by John's social worker at Lynchburg, would not prove to be prophetic. John was discharged in November 1979. He was back at the Training School in four months.

On March 28, 1980, John was admitted to the Social Skills Center at the Training School on an emergency basis. His admission was classified as respite care, and his stay was limited to 21 days. The Social Skills Center specialized in working with people with mental retardation who also needed help with controlling serious behavior problems. John's behavior had become more and more problematic since his discharge. Despite this social worker's optimism, things had apparently not gone well at Kennedy House, the adult home to which he had been transferred. In fact, before being returned to the Training School, John had been committed to Central State Hospital, a psychiatric institution, because he had gotten into a fight with another resident at Kennedy House and had knocked out two of the man's teeth.

Central State is a large mental hospital. John was admitted there on the assumption that his violent behavior might have been the result of a psychotic episode. Examiners there, however, soon diagnosed him as having "no psychosis" and ordered him discharged. Unfortunately, there was no place to send him. Finally, an official in the Office of the Commissioner of Mental Retardation made a special request to the Training Center that John be admitted on a temporary respite basis.

John's behavior while in the Social Skills Center was exemplary. His release summary on April 18 was positive:

> If respite was for an extended period of time, placement on a unit less restrictive than the Social Skills Center [would be recommended] . . . John was noted to interact well with his peers and to be cooperative with staff members. He participated in unit activities and classes.

John was sent from the Training Center to another psychiatric facility. After a short stay there, he was placed in a large adult home in Roanoke. Two years later, he was moved to yet another adult home in that city, where he lived for two and a half years. Then after spending about a month in the Roanoke Valley Psychiatric Center, he was placed in the Burrell Home for Adults, where he was living when I met him. In the six years since he had been "de-institutionalized," John had been placed in nine different settings, all of them institutional in character. The movement toward what was called community-based living for people with intellectual disabilities was a promise that had not become a reality in his life.

John's anger grew more intense with each move. In fact, probably because of his angry outbursts, his diagnosis was changed during this period from mental retardation to mental illness. His many transfers made it very difficult for me to trace his records for this period. It was evident, however, that he became more desperate and disoriented in his behavior, and that he was being perceived by those around him as more and more of a problem.

Despite having been de-institutionalized six years before I came to know him, John had become *re-institutionalized* in the adult home system. In that *re-institutional* system there was no campaign to protect people or to ensure that they were actually in community environments. Ironically, this system was a product of the theory of de-institutionalization that never reached fruition in practice. The small and not-so-small private institutions, operated for profit and created by the de-institutionalization movement, became receptacles for many of the people who were leaving the state-operated mental retardation institutions. They were receptacles with an institutional character but, ironically, with far fewer services and safeguards than had been provided by the institutions from which their residents had been discharged.

VISITING BURRELL HOME

When I first visited John at the Burrell Home in 1987, I was immediately taken with the institutional feel of the place. It had the look and smell of the institutions I had visited for years. More recently, however, the "real" institutions had intentionally made themselves less institutional. They typically had brightly colored walls and windows with curtains or drapes. Pictures, decorations, and variation in décor had supplanted clinical standardization and the hallways of "institutional green."

I had toured several small, publicly supported adult homes and found some of them to be very good places for their residents to live. Others were decent if not inviting. This was my first visit to a large, privately operated (and therefore for-profit) adult home. This was different, appalling different. The Burrell Home was unabashedly institutional. It was drab and full of rough edges.

I tried to visualize the Burrell Home for Adults as I drove the 50 miles from Lynchburg to Roanoke. I knew nothing in advance of its size, history, or organization. When I pulled into the parking lot, however, I was amazed. As I mentioned earlier, I had known the building I saw earlier by another name. I had passed by it often during my childhood and adolescence.

I was born in Roanoke and lived there until I left for college. During those years Roanoke's African American citizens were denied treatment in "white" hospitals. These same people could clean the hospitals, including the one where I was born, but they were refused care in them. I remember as a child passing through the "colored section" of town with my parents on the way to visit relatives and seeing the "colored hospital" on the hill. This was the building I entered on my first visit with John. The Burrell Home was the new manifestation of segregation in an old building that had served that purpose in a different way before.

The word *home* connotes for me a personal place, a place belonging to its inhabitants, and a place where the value of the individual is paramount. A home is where you can be "yourself" and where others know you well. It is a place of closeness between people even when they do not live in complete harmony. The use of the word *home* for an impersonal place, a place of detachment, a place where people have little control over their own lives, is a disturbing contradiction.

The *home* that I visited that Sunday afternoon was nothing like a real home. As I approached the front entrance, I met the gaze of people sitting on the porch and standing on the lawn and around the doorway. As I have found in similar places, they appeared to be surprised, if not startled, when I spoke to them. They seemed to expect that they would be unnoticed, not seen, to be as socially invisible as Ralph Ellison described in *The Invisible Man*. The real problem of being African American, or poor, or old, or having an intellectual disability in the United States lies in not being seen as an individual human being.

Fortunately I had directions from John's social worker for finding John once I was in the building; fortunate because when I walked into the lobby I found no receptionist. It appeared, in fact, that I was the only visitor. I went to the third floor, as the social worker had directed me, and found John's room. He was not there. I inquired at the nurse's station and was told to look for him in the smoking lounge at the end of the hall. There I found several people sitting in the thick smoke of a small room. John was smoking and staring at the floor. The others took little note of me as I entered the room. It was a few seconds before John looked up. When he did I called his name and reminded him of mine. This was the first time we had seen each other since the camping weekend, and so I reminded him that we had met there. He immediately became more animated: Camp Virginia Jaycee is a very happy memory for most who have been there. John seemed happy to have a visitor and was more than willing to give me a tour of Burrell.

As we walked through each of the floors of the old hospital, I came to a sad realization: It was Sunday afternoon, what should be prime time for visitors in a place like this. I had noticed that I was the only visitor in the lobby when I first arrived. Now I realized that I was the only visitor in the entire building. That reality was sharpened for me as we encountered other residents of the home. Many of them wanted to talk, to show me their belongings, particularly pictures. John wanted to keep moving, as if having a visitor was too precious to share.

Months later, an employee of Burrell confided "off the record" that the former "separate but equal" hospital was now the "end of the line" for old and disabled people who were, for the most part, poor and alone. Its residents simply had nowhere else to be and, for almost all of them, nobody who cared. Sunday afternoons were particularly lonely at the Burrell Home.

John and I ended the tour in his room. The only decorations were the crafts he had made at Camp Jaycee. We sat on his bed for a while and talked. I explained that I wanted to know more about his health, and about what should be done if he became very sick. We talked a bit about the no-code order, but I don't think that he fully comprehended what I was talking about. I then asked if he would be willing to sign a form that would allow me to see his records at Burrell. He readily agreed. I am certain that his willingness had more to do with his memory of me at Camp Jaycee than with any real understanding of what I was trying to explain to him. While we were touring the building he had introduced me to several people as the "man from the camp."

John formed his signature slowly and carefully, as I would see him do many times later. His vision was poor even then, and he put his face close to the paper as he signed. When his name was complete he sat back with a look of relief.

I stayed with John for a little longer and then headed back to Lynchburg. As I drove I reflected on the things I had seen that afternoon. For more than a decade I had been lecturing to students on the progress of the de-institutionalization movement and the promise it held for bettering the lives of people with intellectual disabilities. Yet the "community-based" adult home I had just left, a "home" with more than 200 residents, looked more institutional than the state institutions from which many of those residents had been discharged. I arrived at my home, my genuine home, that evening saddened and perplexed.

It would have been easy to condemn a place like the Burrell Home for Adults and decry its manner of operation. It would have been easy, and perhaps satisfying in a way, to blame the problems that John was encountering on particular facilities, programs, and people. To assign blame in such a simplistic, direct fashion is tempting. It is also a mistake. What we really encounter when we examine the life of a person like John Lovelace is a failure of our will as a culture to do anything better for people "at the bottom": those who are old, poor, disabled, and considered to be unproductive and unacceptably dependent; people who are "problems."

ADULT "HOMES"

In 1989 I met a talented young journalist with the *Roanoke Times and World News*. Mike Hudson was just completing an extensive study of the adult home system in Virginia. His findings, published as a series by the newspaper, captured the attention of the public and of professionals and lawmakers within the state and beyond.

Mike traced the beginnings of Virginia's adult homes to what had commonly been called the "old-folks homes" or "rest homes," which were places where elderly people who did not actually require nursing care could go to live out their final years in a quiet and safe environment. These were mostly small, mom-and-pop operations averaging about 24 residents each.

The character of these businesses changed dramatically in the 1970s when state institutions began to open their gates outward, releasing thousands of their residents. As they left these facilities, the resources that had previously been allocated to the institutions by state and federal governments for their care, and that were needed to support their lives in the community, did not follow them. Insufficient numbers of public group homes and other nonprofit living arrangements were established to accommodate the deluge of people who were being de-institutionalized. This void was soon filled through the development of a private, for-profit, adult home industry. Very rapidly these "homes" tripled in number and grew in size as well. By 1989, adult homes ranged from 4 to 600 residents, with an average population of 47. The clients of these "board and care" facilities included elderly and physically ill people, people with intellectual disabilities, and people categorized as mentally ill. A common denominator for most of them, however, was poverty.

Although the homes were run for profit, most derived their revenue from public sources. At the time of Mike Hudson's investigation, each resident who was dependent on federal Supplemental Social Security Income and a state auxiliary grant for her or his care generated $616 per month for the adult home. That translated into about $20.50 per day for staff, food, housing, laundry, recreational programs, and profit for the home. Obviously, if the adult home was to make an attractive profit, the cost per resident had to be kept at a minimum. It is no wonder that the quality of life for the people living in these adult homes quickly became problematic.

Hudson found that licensing for adult homes was based on very low standards. Staffing requirements were also low. Most of the private homes that housed people on public assistance paid their workers minimum wage and provided them with no real training for their jobs. As a result, poorly prepared and inexperienced workers were often responsible for caring for some of the most disabled people in our society. At the time of his study in 1989, Mike Hudson found that approximately 20,000 people were living in 450 adult homes in Virginia. Inspections by state officials of these facilities were infrequent. Homes found to be in violation of meeting the low standards were rarely penalized. The only penalty on the books at the time was revocation of license, and that was rarely done. After all, the basic question was that if a home's license was revoked, where would its residents go? The reality of the disabled and poor as an unwanted class of people was never more clear.

In an earlier and partial account of John Lovelace's plight entitled *Pieces of Purgatory,* I quoted extensively from Mike Hudson's report of his investigation. His words painted a dismaying portrait of what was happening at that time in Virginia's adult homes:

> At Pine Ridge Home for Adults near Farmville, the new owner tangled with a mentally ill resident who refused to leave the kitchen. After the resident kicked him in the stomach, the owner pulled a gun and shot him.
>
> At Arnold's Rest Home near Abingdon, a woman diagnosed with schizophrenia suffered mysteriously broken legs, arms, and ribs. For

several days, the only way she could get from her bedroom to the dining room was by dragging herself across the floor on her bottom.

At Hairston's Home for Adults in Martinsville, the owners admitted a 26-year-old mentally ill man convicted of assaulting a resident at another adult home. A few weeks later, he was charged with murdering a 59-year-old resident by pushing him under scalding water.

At Cardinal Home for Adults in Botetourt County, a mentally ill resident threatened to commit suicide. The owner opened up a medicine cabinet, showed him an unloaded gun, and said: "Go ahead."

Thousands of mentally ill [and mentally retarded] people are in danger of abuse and neglect in adult "board and care" homes across Virginia. They are the victims of a handful of untrained or greedy adult home owners who try to squeeze maximum profits out of their businesses. They are victims of a weak-kneed welfare system that has largely failed to police these operations. And they are victims of a tightfisted state government that has failed to come up with money to improve conditions in poorly run adult homes or find the mentally ill [and retarded] better places to live.[11]

Also in 1989, the congressional Subcommittee on Health and Long-Term Care issued a report called *Board and Care Homes in America: A National Tragedy.* The report estimated that 1 million Americans lived in 68,000 licensed and unlicensed homes. Representative Claude Pepper of Florida, the chairman of the subcommittee, described the care provided in many of these homes as "a tragedy of epic proportions, and a disgraceful failure of public policy." The report emphasized that "regulations for licensed board and care homes are general and some are unenforceable." The following examples were among those highlighted in the subcommittee's report:

In New Mexico, 10 Alzheimer's patients were found bound to their wheelchairs in spite of a law requiring residents to be able to leave the home under emergency situations of their own power. In California, we investigated the murder of seven residents by an ex-felon manager [of the adult home] who then cashed their Social Security checks. In Maryland, an owner continued to house 11 residents in her burned out home—one resident was robbed of all of his possessions. In the District of Columbia, a bedbound elderly woman was found by Subcommittee staff lying in her own urine, begging for food in her roach-infested three-story walk-up room ... In Alabama, a home cited for numerous violations by the Subcommittee, burned down, injuring two of the home's frail elderly residents several days after the visit. In Virginia, we found 11 former mental patients, two of whom required skilled nursing care, warehoused in an old row house.[12]

Has anything dramatic happened since these 1989 reports made public the conditions that existed in adult homes across the country? The tragic answer, as later pages will attest, is that little has changed. Dr. Leete's "complex mutual dependence" as expressed in *Looking Backward* has not been achieved for many people with disabilities in the United States.

CHAPTER 8

Headaches, Smoking, and Fights
Leaving the Home

AMY AND BILL

The following story was told to me by one of my own professors when I was a graduate student. It is about another one of his former students. The story has strengthened and sustained my belief in the critical difference that one person can make in the life of another. It has served to remind me for many years now of the importance of hope, sensitivity, and innovation in the work that we do and in our relationships. I have shared this story with generations of my own students, and I am pleased to share it with you.

Amy, a special education major at a small college, had reached her senior year. She told her advisor that she very much wanted to do her student teaching in a nearby residential facility for adults with mental retardation operated by the state. Amy explained that she preferred that kind of placement rather than student teaching in a public school. Her career goal was to teach adults with developmental disabilities. So her adviser, later my professor, made the arrangements. Amy had also requested that she be assigned to work with people with more severe disabilities. Accordingly, she was given a small number of people with multiple disabilities to work with on an individual basis. She was assigned the task of developing and implementing programs for four people during the 15-week period of her student teaching.

One of the men she was assigned to work with was 35 years old. He had severe cerebral palsy and had been diagnosed as being severely mentally retarded. He was in a wheelchair. He had no control over the movement of his legs. He had some voluntary movement in his arms, but he could not control them very well. He was also able to move some of the muscles in his neck and face. He could not, however, speak. The assumption noted in his records was that he was unable to speak because of his retardation. After Amy started working in the institution, something about this man, whose name was Bill, gave her the impression there was more within him than had been recognized. There was something about the way he moved his eyes, she said. There was something about the way he seemed to react to the things she said to him. She was told by people who worked at the facility that Bill loved being read to. One person commented, "We don't think he understands anything, but he just loves to hear the sound of a voice reading to him." She tried it, and sure enough he did react very positively the minute he saw the book in her hand. "His eyes brightened up," she said.

Bill had been in the institution since he was an infant, having been brought there by parents who felt that they could not take care of him. Amy decided, "Here's a man who has no way of communicating. The only semblance of communication we have is when I watch his face, like when I bring a book into the room and his eyes seem to light up." She later reflected, "I didn't know what that meant, his eyes lighting up. I just wanted to find some way of beginning to teach him to communicate."

BREAKING THROUGH THE SILENCE

In college, Amy had learned about communication boards and how they can be helpful to people who are unable to speak. This was before the development of the various computer keyboards, voice synthesizers, and other augmentative devices that have become so important today in enabling people with disabilities to communicate. Amy's professors had encouraged her to be resourceful and creative, so, she made a very simple communication board one evening after work. She took a big square of cardboard, divided it into four sections, and put a picture in each section. In one section she put a picture of a glass of orange juice, another section had a picture of a bathroom door, the third section had a picture of a book, and the last section contained a picture of a park bench and a tree. Bill had enough movement in his arms and hands to point to these pictures. She wanted to teach him that if he wanted a drink of orange juice, his favorite, he should point to the glass of orange juice on the board. If he needed to use the bathroom, she wanted to teach him that he could point to the picture of the bathroom door, and so on. She brought the board in and demonstrated it to him. Amy placed his hand on the picture of the tree and then she took him outside to the bench, a special place, it seemed, for Bill. She came back inside and put his hand on the picture of the book and then opened a book and read to him. In the process, she thought, "I'll try this for several days and see if I can get him to catch on."

Bill's response, however, proved to be immediate. Amy finished reading and was going to take his hand and point to the glass of orange juice, but he shook his head and grunted. She wasn't sure, but it seemed that he wanted her to continue reading.

She read a few more pages and Bill seemed pleased. When she placed the communication board on his wheelchair again, Bill pointed first to the book and then to the tree. She corrected him by placing his finger on only one of the pictures, the tree. When she gave him another trial, however, he repeated the sequence of touching the book and the tree. She wasn't certain but thought perhaps he was trying to say he wanted to go outside and read. She pushed his wheelchair toward the exit door, and as they passed through it she thought she heard Bill giggle with delight.

THANK YOU

That night Amy made a larger communication board with more pictures, and thus more alternatives. What she saw from Bill the next day was immediate comprehension of how to use the bigger board. She then decided to make a communication board with all the letters of the alphabet, thinking maybe she could begin teaching him to spell simple words. She brought it to work and began using it by trying to teach him the word *book*. She felt that his love of being read to might be very motivating to him in learning *book* as his first word. She held his finger and pointed to B, then to O, to another O, and finally to K. She repeated the word *book* and put his hand on the one she had been reading from.

She then encouraged Bill to point to the letters on his own. His finger went immediately to the letter T. She corrected him by placing his finger again on the B and calling out the name of the letter. When he was again given the freedom to point, however, his finger went in a seemingly deliberate manner to the T. Amy decided to let him proceed. Bill in a slow, labored, and careful way, pointed to the sequence of letters that communicated to her his message of choice. He said to his teacher, T H A N K Y O U. Amy was astounded.

FINDING A VOICE AND VISIBILITY

Bill had never been taught to read or write; he had never been given academic instruction of any kind. Apparently over the years, however, when people read to him, Bill watched carefully. He had taught himself to read. Amy began to work with Bill on the communication board with greater intensity. She spent her evenings and weekends listening to him through his pointing to letters. He spoke with her about a lifetime of unexpressed perceptions and silent frustrations. Once she understood how deeply he could communicate with the spelling board, she told others at the institution. Many of them said, "There must be some misunderstanding; Bill is severely retarded."

She finally convinced a psychologist to watch as she asked questions of Bill, to which he responded by pointing to the letters of the alphabet. The psychologist was absolutely amazed. He decided to give Bill some sections of an IQ test through his communication board. Not only did he find that Bill was not severely mentally retarded, the psychologist estimated that his IQ fell into the superior range. He had been locked into his body for 35 years and treated as if he were severely retarded. He had no way of telling the world he wasn't. Amy had given him a key — she had given him a means of communicating and demonstrating the depth of his comprehension and insight.

By this time, Amy was nearing the completion of her student teaching. She asked special permission, however, to remain at the facility that summer and work with Bill. This was allowed. As a result of Amy's efforts and the world that had opened to him through the communication board, Bill moved out of the institution the next year and into a group home. Amy continued to work with him and taught him to type on an electric typewriter. It was a slow process, but he mastered it. A new freedom of expression came to him with the keyboard.

Bill developed friendships in the community that surrounded the group home. He became an active member of a local church. He loved going to community theater performances. He was invited to join a civic organization. Unfortunately, he died of a stroke when he was in his late forties. It is sad to think that until he was 35 years old he was treated as severely disabled by everyone who knew him. He had so few years of liberation from his disability. His friend and teacher Amy, however, found a way of helping him break through, so for at least 10 years of his life he was recognized as a person, not as a disability.

We all need to be very careful with the assumptions we make about people, and extremely careful about the assumptions we make about people who have trouble communicating. We often jump to conclusions when people can't communicate effectively, and we sometimes have lower expectations of them. Bill and Amy come to my mind when I am tempted to make judgments about the potentials of others. I'm glad Bill found a voice. I'm glad that I know their story.

SMOKING VIOLENCE

John was admitted to the Burrell Home for Adults on October 15, 1985. As I explained earlier, this was his ninth "home" in six years. The records indicate that he seemed to be doing well during his first few days at Burrell. He was described as adjusting quickly. It was also mentioned that he was enthusiastic about going back to work at the sheltered workshop where he had worked earlier while living in another adult home. The assessment of his first nine days at Burrell was that he caused "no management problems." The nurse in charge of this first progress report said, "John appears to be doing well. [He] states he likes Burrell and staff. He states he is ready to return to TMW [the sheltered workshop] . . . Appointment with . . . counselor Oct. 28 [at] 10:00, 'Anger Management' group to start November 5, 9-10:00 . . . "

From these initial notes it sounds like things were going well for John. His adjustment to the placement sounds good. His anticipation of returning to work seems like a positive sign. The fact that he had been registered for involvement in a program to help him manage his anger looks good.

The anger management group was a service that had been arranged through the public agency responsible for providing mental health services in the community to people diagnosed as having mental health problems. A similar agency, mental retardation services, was responsible for meeting the needs of mentally retarded people in the community. Both agencies were subsumed under and directed by a regional governing board.

During the era of most activity under the rubric of de-institutionalization, Virginia was divided into regions for the purpose of serving those people who were leaving the state's institutions and those who earlier would have been entering institutions. In each region the administrative structure created to provide services was known as the community services board. Thus, in the Lynchburg area there was the Central Virginia Community Services Board, and in Roanoke there was the Community Services Board of the Roanoke Valley.

By the time that John was moved to Burrell Home the perception of his problems and the change of his diagnosis to schizophrenia had resulted in his case being managed by Mental Health Services of the Roanoke Valley. His needs were no longer being perceived in terms of retardation, and therefore he was not receiving any assistance from Mental Retardation Services.

By the summer of 1985, a few months before his admission to Burrell Home, the focus of his case had become his anger. The question of how his anger related to his mental retardation was not being addressed. His records at Mental Health Services speak primarily to his need for anti-convulsive medication, his aggressive and violent behavior, and his diagnosis as a schizophrenic. Excerpts from his medical notes at Mental Health Services are instructive in this regard. These notes were written by a consulting psychiatrist who was seeing him under the auspices of Mental Health Services at the time:

7/10/85: Seen with therapist . . . violent episodes in the last week are reported, including punching others in the face with little provocation. Hospitalization is recommended on a Mental Health Warrant.

8/14/85: Since last visit, John had an uneventful admission to Roanoke Rehab under my care where he showed no active problems in that setting. He was discharged after a brief weekend stay essentially. Today there are still reports of some irritable behavior on his part that may be provoked by other residents. I am shifting his Mellaril medication so that he gets more during the daytime when these occur. He will now be taking 100mg., 4 times a day. His Dilantin and Phenobarb are renewed unchanged . . .

9/11/85: Seen today for a one week follow-up emergency appointment. Last week, he was started on Amitriptyline to see if an antidepressant could reduce his irritability. As is sometimes seen in schizophrenia, the antidepressant had the opposite effect and increased his irritability. I am therefore stopping it and going to a more sedative regimen of Thorazine 600 mg. per day . . .

2/12/86: . . . John is doing well at the Burrell Home. There are no complaints. His medicine has not been changed since his hospitalization. It is renewed unchanged . . . He is friendly and in good spirits.

Things were not actually going as smoothly as the psychiatrist's perception would indicate. John began to experience some difficulties early on in his experience at Burrell. Things did not begin to become critical, however, until May 1986. The daily notes made by the nurses in charge of each shift are particularly revealing of what John was doing at that time and how it was perceived by the nursing staff. The notes for the afternoon of May 26 show that John was seriously hurt during that nursing shift. The notes that follow also offer a further explanation of what happened to him:

5/10/86, 2:10 pm—Called to floor from lunch by resident. Arrived to find John lying on floor and bleeding from back of head. Ambulance had been called . . . Responsive to name but was slightly dazed. 2:25 pm —Ambulance arrived-head bandaged-cervical collar applied-back board used. 2:25 pm—Transported to Roanoke Memorial Hospital . . .

5/10/86 Resident was involved in a fight with [another] . . . resident earlier today and sent to emergency room. He returned . . . very calm and quiet. Stitches were needed and given at emergency room . . . Resident is at present time sitting in smoking room creating no problems, will observe. 8:00—Resident still sitting in smoking room, alert and aware of surroundings. 10:00—Asleep in room. Aroused easily, aware of name, place and date.

I have no evidence of what caused the fight which led to his injury. There is not even an indication of who the fight was with. After having given considerable study to John and his behavior, however, I feel confident that the fight concerned cigarettes. Either John was out of cigarettes and was trying to find some way to get one, or he felt at risk for losing a cigarette. John was heavily addicted to tobacco. This is not at all unusual for people who have been institutionalized. Cigarettes were traditionally the one officially sanctioned "vice" among disabled people placed in institutions. Normal sex drives were never acknowledged in mental health and mental retardation facilities and, therefore, no healthy provision was made for their expression. Drinking was never allowed. Smoking, however, was not only allowed, it was encouraged. Smoking was used as a means of behavior control. Residents who did what they were told were rewarded with cigarettes and/or more frequent opportunities to smoke them. Cigarettes were held by authority figures and parceled out one at a time for compliant behavior.

In the current social climate which emphasizes "smoke free environments," the smokiest places I found in the 1990s were the smoking areas of adult homes, institutions, and other places where adults with developmental disabilities lived and worked. I say this as a former smoker who has become increasingly sensitive to the presence of cigarette smoke. Cigarettes, and coffee, were the currency of adult homes and similar places. People *lived* for them. They had nothing else to look forward to, so coffee and cigarettes "drove" the cultures of adult homes. Favors and friendship were controlled by the cigarette trade, and to a lesser extent, coffee. Monthly allowances were thought of in terms of how many cigarettes they could buy. Visitors from the outside were thought of in terms of the opportunity for a little extra money for cigarettes.

Although there were obviously exceptions, cigarettes and coffee dominated the moment-to-moment consciousness of most people in adult homes. John was more addicted than most people in those settings. He became very anxious when he started to think about running out. Again, I understand this well because of the years that I was addicted myself. Unfortunately, John's ability to secure that next pack was much more problematic for him than it was for me, or for most smokers. In the face of nicotine cravings that he could not satisfy, he fell apart and would strike out at others.

A sampling from the daily nursing notes indicates how problematic his smoking addiction was for John at Burrell Home:

6/8/86—June Summary: Resident sleeps majority of night on 11-7 [the shift]. However, on occasion does stay in smoking lounge all night. Will get upset if he is out of cigarettes and throws chairs and uses abusive language . . .

6/9/86-10:00 pm—John was sitting in dayroom and Sherman . . . came up and asked John to give him a cigarette. John said no and Sherman got mad and hit John in the face and head. Then they began to hit each other. Sherman knocked John to the floor and began to kick John on the leg. John kicked him back . . .

2/23/87-At 2:45 am—resident Lovelace came to desk demanding cigarettes. After resident was informed that he did not have any smoking materials, he cursed, slammed chairs, kicked doors and pounded the plexiglass of the nurse's station with his fists. Resident was asked to return to quarters. Lovelace replied, " . . . not until I get a cigarette." Incident reported to LPN on duty. Resident quiet while nurse on floor. Immediately after departure of duty nurse, resident began cursing and picked up several chairs in the smoking lounge. Lovelace demanded personal smoking materials belonging to staff, but was denied due to his behaviors. Resident responded by charging up to nurse's station with a chair as if to break down the plexiglass around the desk. The nurse on duty was notified again.

It may seem a simplistic explanation, but I am convinced that John's angry outbursts, and the resultant injuries and difficulties that these brought to him, were precipitated for years by the complications of his cigarette addiction and by his headaches. From his earliest records there are reoccurring notations of his complaining of headaches. These complaints often preceded his episodes of disruptive behavior. I talked with John about this, but he was unable to explain to me about his headaches; how they made him feel and how long they lasted. I wondered if he had been experiencing migraine headaches, or something like them, all of his life. The idea that perhaps he had suffered great pain that he was unable to comprehend himself or articulate to others was very disturbing to me. I asked that attention be paid to this possibility during a physical examination, but nothing was found or reported. Another example from John's records at Burrell Home is illustrative of his headache problems:

> 9/20/86—Sept. Summary
> Resident has been having problems with headaches of late, CAT scan among other testings done, is also encouraged to wear glasses which helps with redness of eyes . . . stays in around Home [rather than going off the grounds for organized activities?] now that he is having difficulty with headaches . . . Resident has frequent outbursts of anger. Can become violent at times. Likes to smoke and drink coffee . . . No plans to discharge at this time.

John was becoming more and more of a problem. In addition to his angry outbursts, however, other difficulties were beginning to be noticed. In October of 1986 a nurse noted that his gait was becoming worse. He had always walked with a limp and shuffled due to his cerebral palsy, but it was noticed that he was now leaning forward much more markedly. He was also beginning to stumble more frequently as he moved about the home. In February of 1987 he was described as "becoming increasingly worse. John sits down when he is to stand, is starting to wet clothing. Gait is not as stable as in past months." This difference in his gait and coordination may have been related to eye difficulties that he was having at the time, which were not recognized as being serious but which were treated several months later. Whatever the case, the nurse's notes do reflect an image of John as a weaker, more disabled person.

THE ORDER

On March 17 a licensed practical nurse reported on John's condition and seemingly initiated the request for a "no-code" order for him. On a request to the consulting physician at Burrell Home she wrote, "Resident is sleeping most of the days and complains of severe headaches . . . When he is not at work [at the sheltered workshop] he is in bed most of day. Appears more lethargic . . . request follow-up of CAT scan . . . also written excuse for work and an order for 'No Code'." After examining John the physician wrote on the bottom of the form, "Please advise of patient's next of kin."

The summary entry in his records for March says, "Resident has appeared to regress—resting more with frequent headaches—has not been going to workshop regularly—Remains continent of bowels and bladder—Appetite good—Less frequent episodes of outbursts noted-dHas ordered a 'No Code' status due to condition at this time."

John was treated for his eye ailment in late April. He must have felt better physically after this treatment. His angry outbursts, however, came back with a vengeance. On April 22 he exploded, as always, in the smoking lounge. No reason was noted for it, but I am certain it was the same, a perceived or real inequity in cigarette dealings. John threw chairs and ashtrays. He pushed another resident against the wall. He defied the staff.

Over the next four months these episodes continued, always in the smoking lounge. On one occasion John was handcuffed and taken to an emergency psychiatric center. He stayed there for two weeks and was returned to Burrell.

John's swan song at the Burrell Home for Adults came on September 23, 1987. The circumstances are no surprise: "Resident was in day-room smoking—an argument aroused between him and Wendell . . . When we entered the day room . . . he struck another resident . . . "

The same day: "Helen . . . states that John hit her in the eye for coffee."

And then the entry that would end his stay and Burrell: "John was told today he is getting 2 weeks notice to move, Mental Health Services—Mental Retardation notified."

CHAPTER 9

Defining Disability Up and Down

In an earlier chapter I compared the wording in the movie with that in the book *Forrest Gump.* Another distinctly different portrayal of the character Forrest Gump in the movie contrasted to that in Winston Groom's book comes in the experience he has while being inducted into the army. The movie dialogue between Forrest and a drill sergeant is:

Drill Sergeant: Gump! What's your sole purpose in this army?

Forrest Gump: To do whatever you tell me, drill sergeant!

Drill Sergeant: Goddammit Gump! You're a Goddamn genius! This is the most outstanding answer I have ever heard. You must have a Goddamn IQ of 160. You are Goddamn gifted, Private Gump . . .

In Groom's book the exchange between the sergeant and Forrest is quite different. Forrest and his mother report to a U.S. Army Induction Center, and his description of his encounter with the sergeant is:

The big ole sergeant be hollerin and yellin at everybody and momma goes up to him and says, "I don't see how you can take my boy—cause he's a *idiot,*" but the sergeant just looked back at her and say, "Well, lady, what do you think all these other people is? Einsteins?"[1]

There are many jokes about the character and the purpose of intellect in military environments. References to the term "military intelligence" as being an oxymoron, being self-contradictory, are commonplace. What is not commonly understood, however, is the ambivalence that has existed for almost a century regarding the meaning of measured intelligence and the need for troops in times of war. This was particularly true in the United States during the two "great wars."

WORLD WAR I AND THE FIRST "GREAT" TESTING

During the summer of 1917, the psychologist Henry Goddard participated in a project that was to have far-reaching social consequences in American culture. He was enlisted by fellow psychologist Robert Yerkes (who shared his interest in both mental testing and the heredity of intelligence) to help in the design and construction of mental tests for the U.S. Army. The tests were to be used for the classification of recruits during World War I. The instruments were titled the Army Alpha and Beta tests. The Alpha was a written test for use with literate recruits, and the Beta used pictures to test those who could not read. More than a million and a half men were given these tests by the end of the war.[2]

The results of this massive screening of the intelligence of American males were published in several army reports beginning in 1918. Goddard presented data indicating that 45 percent of all the recruits had mental ages below 13 years. On this basis, he projected that 45 percent of the entire population, if tested, would be classified no higher in intellect than that of morons (otherwise known as "high-grade" defectives). He concluded, given that the average American adult had only the mentality of a 13-year-old child, almost half of the population was even less intelligent. Therefore, he argued, the prospects for universal education for American children was poor, since 45 percent did not have the capacity to go beyond elementary school, and 70 percent could not be expected to be successful beyond the eighth grade.[3]

There is little evidence, however, that the Alpha and Beta tests had a significant impact on the actual selection and assignment decisions made by the military during World War I. In fact, one report indicated that examining boards at induction centers often accepted the "high grade moron" even though he had been rejected by a psychologist on the basis of test results.[4]

By the end of the war an Army regulation had been issued specifying that " . . . a feebleminded individual who has the intelligence of a child of eight years may be accepted to service in the Army."[5] This may be an indication that soldiers who had been tested and classified as feebleminded had, in contradiction to the label, performed successfully during the war. Scheerenberger points out the irony that following the war many soldiers who had earlier escaped from institutions, and who served with honor in the military, were recommitted to those same institutions upon their return to civilian life.[6]

WAR, TESTING, AND EUGENICS

Although Army Alpha and Beta testing had limited impact on the actual selection of soldiers in World War I, the influence of the tests in political and social policy arenas was enormous. Goddard, Yerkes, and others sounded alarms based on the test scores and called for eugenic measures to control the further dilution of the American intellect. These assertions led to increasing numbers of people being institutionalized and sterilized. The data from the testing of World War I recruits also fueled the push for restrictions on immigration and fortified the arguments for racial segregation and for miscegenation laws.[7] Indeed, the World War I testing contributed greatly to what James Trent has termed the "invention" of the feeble mind.[8] In many ways the interwar period of the next two decades was the zenith of eugenic thinking and its great impact on people who were controlled and contained in its name—those who were believed to be a threat to society and to have little to contribute to the common good.

It is interesting to examine how eugenic influences began to change in dramatic ways during the next "great war." The powerful message of hereditary mental defectiveness was being articulated with authority at the moment of the first involvement of the United States in World War II. Edgar Doll, one of the most influential voices in intellectual disabilities at the time, was convinced that it was largely an atavistic condition, a reversion to a more primitive stage of physical and cultural development that reflected an earlier step on the ladder of human evolution. These people, it was argued, were not suited for living in a modern world and institutionalization was best for them and for society.[9] It likely came as quite a surprise to the superintendents of some of the institutions when they found that parolees and escapees from their facilities—people classified as being hopelessly mentally deficient—were successfully enlisting in the military.[10]

WORLD WAR II, RETARDATION, AND THE "GREATEST GENERATION"

World War II brought a need for men that overshadowed inductee selection according to strict and inflexible criteria. At the beginning of the war as many as 1,000 men per day were sworn into the military. Soon the army was accepting enlistees who could not read or write, as long as they were able to follow simple orders in English. [11,12] Stephen Gelb presents an analysis that clearly shows the military was not likely to label a man as mentally retarded and thereby lose a soldier. These were the same men who had been assigned this label for institutional commitment or special education placement for years. The emergency of war and the shortage of recruits changed the perception of the competence of these men. To put this difference of perceived competence into an easily understood context, Gelb points out that African-American males were almost 100 times more likely to be identified as mentally retarded by schools in some southern states in the 1970s than by the military in World War II. [13]

A report in 1946 of males who had been described as mentally retarded and enrolled in special classes before the war, and yet who made significant contributions as soldiers during World War II, is revealing of how they were perceived differently in two different social contexts. Their recorded IQs ranged from 52 to 83, and they had received what was referred to as "limited academic training." They had attended special classes for an average of four years and nine months, and 80% had left school as soon as they reached 16, when they were no longer required by law to attend. In 1943 it was found that almost 55 percent of these young men were on active duty with the military. Another 15 percent or so were working in defense-related jobs or were waiting to be drafted. The report observed, "In brief, it may be said that they were found to be a self-respecting group who had responded in creditable fashion to the war emergency." [14]

MENTAL RETARDATION AND SAVING DEMOCRACY: PREDICTIONS AND REFLECTIONS

In an address to the American Association on Mental Deficiency in 1944, Edgar Doll, then director of the Department of Research at The Training School at Vineland, continued with his pessimistic view of the role of people with intellectual disabilities in the war effort. While not citing data or references, he said:

> Many mental defectives have entered the armed services by one route or another, some with the approval of some of us, and some over the protest of others. It is safe to say that the earnest hopes of the former have been seriously disappointed, while the grave fears of the others have not proved entirely justified. The mental defective at best rarely makes a first-class fighter. [15]

While equally pessimistic about the promise of men who had been classified as having mental retardation as soldiers, the views of other institutional professionals of the war and eugenics included the following remarks:

> War takes the fit and leaves the unfit. The eugenical impact will tell the future generations when the moron is left unsupervised at home to beget the succeeding generations of our citizens. Logical reasoning can only tell us that such a course results in lowering the general intellectual level of the people of the nation and will argue more strongly than ever for the inauguration of a more definite control plan for the prevention of the defective stocks.
>
> In conclusion, physically strong and mentally stable men of moron classification who are willing and anxious to serve in some phase of the war effort should be inducted . . . I surmise that Germany now would like to have a million or two men like our stable morons to throw against the Russian lines.[16]

Contrary to these presumptions and cynical views, however, are the available records of the service of men who had been institutionalized earlier in their lives and who then served in the American military during World War II. A number of detailed accounts of their service are available. A few excerpts are illustrative of the contributions of these men. A report of "boys" with a connection to the Elwyn State School included these comments:

> The Tech. Sgt., two Staff Sgts. (I.Q. 59 and 75), and two Sgts. (I.Q. 74 and 91), are pre-Pearl Harbor men representing the Air Force, Infantry, Field Artillery, and Medical Corps. The single post-Pearl Harbor Staff Sgt. (I.Q. 60) is an instructor in the Army Air Force. The Corporal (I.Q. 81) won his rating shortly after enlisting because he had worked as a skilled mechanic during the time that he dodged selective service by assuring his draft board that he was feeble-minded.[17]

Another comment not only portrays the success of formerly institutionalized men in the war effort, it also expresses an early skepticism regarding the validity of intelligence testing in the global prediction of abilities and life outcomes:

> Three of our boys have been promoted to sergeants, several have been made corporals, and one is seaman, first class.[18]

It is quite apparent that in the selection of inductees for Army training, too much reliance cannot be placed upon the psychometric test.

A larger study of the issue of intellectual disabilities in World War II confirms these descriptions. In assessing the performance of a group of 8,000 people previously identified as "mental defectives," the author found that half of the group adjusted successfully, performed their jobs well, gained new skills, fortified their personality structure, and became functioning members of the military group.[19] Perhaps more importantly, the author summarizes the importance of the study by stating:

> We submit, in the light of our survey, the conclusion that a peacetime society and industry can no longer consider the mental defective as useless ... what a potential force of manpower now returns to civilian status! It is our hope that society and industry can recognize the importance of understanding, fortifying, and utilizing to the ultimate, a human being whose assets heretofore have been considered EXPEND-ABLE ITEMS.[20]

What a tragedy, indeed, that these words were not heeded. The place of people characterized as having mental retardation in American society went unchanged. The lessons that the "Great Wars" offered went unlearned.

IN REGARD TO MY SON JOHN

On November 3, 1948, John Lovelace's foster mother wrote to the superintendent of the Lynchburg Training School and Hospital. He had only been admitted in October, but in her letter it is apparent that she was anxious to have him back home with her. Mrs. Hunter would repeatedly request that John be allowed to come home on "furlough" or "parole." As a result, and as was pointed out earlier, John actually spent very little time in the institution during his first commitment there. Her November letter, however, does depict a concern that she had for John and a reason, probably the primary reason, why she wanted him to be committed in the first place. Again, I have not edited the language of her letters but have left them to reflect the character of a woman with little education but a great depth of compassion for her foster son:

> In regard to my son John R. Lovelace a patient there I was down to see him 31 of October and found him very Home sick and seems to be unable to adjust him self in any way and [I] have allways new his General Health means a better mind. Now would you be so kind as to Paroll this Boy to me as soon as he has had the necessary medical treatment such as being Stirrel and having his Tonisal and Adinois removed. I kindly would like for you to do that much while he is there. I am unable to have that done here. Reason—mostly lack of funds to pay off with but

you can do this for us and Paroll him in our care I will try to get his General health up again and he might go on sevrile years with[out] giving any trouble Will I need any one signature other than myself and Husband I don't want to come down there unprepared to sign papers.
     Yours truly, Mr. & Mrs. W I Hunter

It is clear from her letter that Mrs. Hunter felt that sterilization was an important health measure for John. It is interesting that she grouped it with removal of his tonsils and adenoids as a preventative procedure that would be good for him, and that she could not otherwise afford to provide for him. Her attitude in this regard was reflective of what had become the conventional wisdom of the time concerning those who were considered retarded or otherwise incompetent: The greatest threat to society, and to themselves, that these people pose is the threat of reproduction of bad traits, and also the reproduction of those traits in children that they are patently unable to care for properly.

It is very likely that Mrs. Hunter viewed sterilization as something that she, as a good mother, had a responsibility to seek for her son. It was something that he needed that she couldn't afford. By appealing to the Training School for it, she was doing the best she could for her child. Of course, the same conventional wisdom prevailed at the Lynchburg Training School and Hospital. A staff meeting of physicians, psychologists, and social workers convened on April 4, 1949, concerning John. Their report ended with the comment: "Eugenic sterilization is emphatically recommended." Mrs. Hunter's request was honored, and the staff recommendation was followed. On July 18, 1949, John was sterilized.

EUGENICS AND INSTITUTIONS

Eugenics was a movement that claimed to be based on scientific principles. It gained widespread acceptance in medicine, genetics, and the social sciences during the early part of the twentieth century. It heavily influenced both politicians and practitioners in all of the human service fields. As a result, several generations of poor people, people with disabilities, and people otherwise socially disadvantaged felt the impact of the practices that were developed based on this philosophy. Basically eugenics, sometimes called the "science of race improvement," advocated the reproductive control of people who were deemed to have poor genetic makeup. The idea was that certain people carried "bad seeds" for mental retardation, mental illness, epilepsy, alcoholism, criminality, and even poverty. The primary means for controlling the reproduction of those deemed genetically inferior was sterilization. Eugenics enthusiasts also felt that people of "good stock" should be encouraged to have large families and thereby pass on their genetic superiority to increasing numbers of offspring.

This view, that it is not too much to ask for someone's reproductive rights to be sacrificed to the greater good of all, was reflected in the majority opinion in the Supreme Court decision in the case of Buck v. Bell, written by Oliver Wendell Holmes. Holmes referred to compulsory vaccination as a requirement for the protection of others against the transmission of disease, and he drew a parallel with compulsory sterilization as a reasonable requirement for the protection of others against the transmission of social and moral threats. He also argued that it was best for the class of people most affected because it was more humane than the eventual punishments those born defective would receive for their antisocial acts.[21]

The expansion of institutions for people classified as mentally retarded and mentally ill during the first half of this century was rationalized in the same way as involuntary sterilization. People were institutionalized because, it was argued and accepted, it was best for them and for society. It was even argued that mentally disabled people had a "right" to be institutionalized. In an article written in 1916 by Joseph Mastin, the Secretary of the Virginia Board of Charities and Corrections, and published in the *Journal of Psycho-Asthenics* entitled "The New Colony Plan for the Feeble-Minded," included the following observations:

> ... The right of the defective, then, is not the right to live as he pleases, but the right to live the fullest life possible under proper guidance. But the right is just as sacred as our own and we must see that he has it; to deny it is a social crime as well as a violation of the commandment, "Thou shalt love they neighbor as thyself."
>
> ... Therefore, while mental defectives are clearly not entitled to the rights of normal persons, it is indisputable that society is under obligations to give them such training as may be suited to their needs and capacities ...
>
> ... As a rule, mental defectives are descended from the poorer classes, and for generations their people have lived in homes having few conveniences. To expect them to be contented in a great city institution with its up-to-date furnishings and equipment, and its strict routine, is unreasonable. They find little comfort in steam heat and polished floors; and the glare of our electric lights too often adds to their restlessness.

...when the State shall demand that those in charge of her degenerate and helpless people shall see that they live happy and useful lives and that procreation by them is rendered impossible: then we can look forward with confidence to the coming of an era when feeblemindedness will become extinct, mental disease will vanish and crime and pauperism will be reduced to a minimum. Then, and not until then, shall we get a clearer vision of the new heaven and the new earth wherein dwelleth righteousness.[22]

The growth of institutions for people classified as mentally disabled was dramatic during the period from the turn of the century through the 1950s. More institutions and larger institutions became the hallmarks of the integrity of state programs for the care of people who were judged to be mentally retarded or mentally ill and in need of care and protection. Unfortunately, these institutions also became repositories for people who clearly did not require institutionalization. Availability of the institutions made it easy and convenient to place people there who might have been able to live independently in society but who required a bit more attention or help than the average person. As more spaces were made available in institutions, people were found to fill them. As more people came, more spaces were created. Not only were people with mild disabilities that did not require confinement sent to institutions, but also people who were not intellectually disabled at all.

As I discussed in my book, *Minds Made Feeble,* American society in the early twentieth century took note of what appeared to be growing numbers of people who were vagrants, criminals, prostitutes, alcoholics, and other social undesirables. Their negative traits were interpreted to be evidence of their mental deficiency, and it was decided that they needed to be hidden away from the rest of the culture. In many cases, people who were simply unwanted by anyone, people who were social nuisances in some way, and people who were without advocates to protect them found themselves in institutions. Sometimes they were inaccurately assigned a diagnostic label of mental retardation or mental illness, and sometimes not even the formality of a diagnostic designation was assigned.[23]

I have reviewed many records of people who were admitted to an institution for persons who were mentally retarded, and lived there for decades, whose files designated them as "Not retarded." The staff of the institutions, and sometimes the people committed there themselves, knew the reason they were there was that they were simply unwanted; they were surplus persons who society had decided to warehouse. The warehousing was done, again, in the name of protection. Protection of society from the person who was considered a deviant, and protection of the vulnerable deviant from the harsh realities of competitive social living were the dominant rationales for institutionalization.

Colonies, training schools, hospitals, and developmental centers, whatever they were called, became closed institutions. They have sometimes been referred to as "total institutions." They were often intentionally self-sufficient: they raised their own crops, had their own dairies, and sewed their own clothes. They were almost always walled off from the rest of society. Doors and gates were locked. The residents were called patients but they were often dressed more like inmates. I have visited many institutional buildings with bars on the doors and windows, restraining devices on the walls, and slots in doors for the passing of food trays. The impression I have had at times is that institutions of this era had schizoid personalities. They truly did not know if they were hospitals or prisons, or something in between. The personality of the institution, however, was often more clear to the patients. They often learned to play the game and to survive as best they could. At least there was a sense of certainty in the routine and the predictability of these places.

DE-INSTITUTIONALIZATION

Institutional certainty and predictability ended for hundreds of thousands of people beginning in the 1970s. This change came with a national movement that became known as de-institutionalization. The clearing out of people who had lived for decades in institutions commenced. Its impact would prove to be as dramatic as the increase in institutionalization had been earlier in the century.

The primary goal of the movement was admirable, and it was one that I believed in and supported as a teacher, graduate student, and professor. That goal, to help people who do not really require institutional care to have lives that are as normal as possible in local communities, is still embraced by most people who are advocates for the rights and welfare of people who live with intellectual disabilities. It sounded like a wonderful goal. It sounded like a curative measure for the institutional ills of the past. When it has been done with the correct kinds of planning, preparation, and resources, it resulted in much more full, free, and decent lives for those who have benefitted from it.

Two flaws plagued the de-institutionalization movement, however. One flaw was that financial and service resources often did not follow people from institutions to the community. The dollars that had been used for years to house, feed, clothe, and otherwise care for people in institutions did not follow them in proportional amounts to support their transition to life in local communities. In most cases, community support services were created to provide for the needs that had earlier been most often met in segregated institutional settings. Social workers, psychologists, and other professional personnel were employed by state governments to meet the needs of de-institutionalized people in community placements, but the numbers were never adequate.

As I reflect on my own experiences over several decades, I have consistently seen competent and caring professionals stretched to the limit by case loads that are impossible to manage. I have also seen, again and again, salary levels for these positions set so low that it is very difficult to attract and keep people with adequate training and experience. I must add that I have also known fine people who have dedicated their professional lives to enhancing the community life of persons with disabilities against all odds. They have worked for low salaries, often under adverse circumstances and with little recognition, and they have made all the difference in the lives of those for whom they advocate. They have been truly heroic in their efforts, and my admiration for them is immense.

The other flaw in the de-institutionalization movement was that there were inadequate efforts made at the state and national level to develop appropriate places in communities for the people who left institutions to live.

A FLAWED GOOD INTENTION

Given the focus of this book on examining the effects of social policy on people with intellectual abilities through the life experiences of John Lovelace, I think it is most important to look at what de-institutionalization meant at the facility from which he was reintroduced to the community after 25 years of institutional life. My colleague Dr. Ed Polloway at Lynchburg College and I analyzed discharge records from the Central Virginia Training Center (formerly the Lynchburg Training School and Hospital) from the year 1969 through 1989. We hoped to come to an understanding of the patterns of discharge as they related to the age, level of retardation, length of institutionalization, and other factors that might reflect changes across this period in national and state laws, policies, and professional trends. It was challenging work. More than 2,300 persons were discharged from the facility during this period.

One interesting finding is that when we looked at all of the discharges for that period as a whole, the word de-institutionalization was a misnomer for about 40 percent of the people who left the institution. Although these people may have eventually found their way to something other than an institutional setting, their initial discharge was to another institution. These persons were discharged to either regional mental retardation centers, psychiatric facilities, or geriatric facilities. In every case these were state-operated institutions. Nearly 2 percent of the people who were officially discharged during this period were classified as "escapees." These were people who disappeared while on parole or furlough and were thereby lost to the system. I suspect many of these people genuinely did find a better life in the community on their own. A little less than half a percent of those discharged were actually released to the criminal justice system. These were, for the most part, people who were convicted of crimes while on parole, furlough, or while having escaped from the institution. Another 30 percent of the people who left Central Virginia Training Center between 1969 and 1989 were discharged to their own care or that of their families. In these cases, there was usually very little evidence of a bridge of care or preparation. In some cases, it appears they were sent to the community but that little was done to prepare them for the community or to prepare the community for them.[24]

About 15 percent of the institution's discharged residents did in fact leave to go into government-sponsored and community-based programs and facilities. These included group homes, halfway houses, intermediate care facilities (intermediate here meaning a level of care intermediate between institutionalization and community living), supervised apartments, work training programs, and foster homes. Our study, then, indicated that about 15 percent of the people who left in the name of de-institutionalization went directly into community living programs of some sort. We can only hope that more people actually arrived in appropriate community programs eventually after making an initial stop somewhere else, but we have no data to tell us if this was the case.

Finally, almost 13 percent of those leaving the institution between 1969 and 1989 were discharged to private, and primarily profit-driven, adult homes or nursing homes. There were certainly many people who also found their way to these for-profit adult and nursing homes after an initial stop in one of the other placements already described.[25] It is apparent that during this period adult homes became a growth industry. Unfortunately, they also became a dumping ground for unwanted people of every description and diagnosis. I have visited a number of these homes and have consistently found them, as I mentioned earlier, to be populated by a mixture of elderly people, people with intellectual disabilities, people with other disabilities, and people who are otherwise damaged and/or alone. So often the common denominator is that they are simply poor, weak, unwanted, and unable to defend themselves against a social environment that wants them out of the way.

So, John Lovelace left the institution that had become his home and where he knew how to play the game, how to survive, and where he had a few friends among its staff. He left to go to environments where he would fare much worse. His behavior, as discussed earlier, would deteriorate, and each new adult home placement would be a step down the ladder for him. He finally found himself living in a "home" with 200 other unwanted people, where his very life would be counted as not worth saving. De-institutionalization and community placement did not work for John. I fear the irony of his history at truly having a chance to "live and work . . . just like all other men in our country" is one shared by thousands of others.

I have had numerous conversations over the years with friends and colleagues about the motivations of people who were involved in actions that today seem shameful in the effects they had on lives that we would consider to be undeserving of the harm that was done to them. Were the people who led the movement to increase the number and size of institutions, those who worked to remove more and more people from society because of perceived defects, calloused toward the humanity of those that they sought to commit to those institutions? Were the people who designed and implemented involuntary sterilization laws in this country fascists? The answer to these questions is, of course, no.

Studying these movements has led me to the realization that these were causes taken up by people with the best of personal and philosophical intentions in most cases. The advocates of involuntary sterilization were often people who also spoke out strongly for more equitable treatment of people in racial and ethnic minority groups. Among them I found individuals who were ahead of their time in calling for greater social equality for women. Those who helped promote institutionalization of people with intellectual disabilities included people who were recognized humanitarians and philanthropists. The damage done to people by needless institutionalization and unjustified sterilization was not their intent, but it happened. I am sure some of the advocates of these movements would have been shocked at the consequences of their actions if they had lived long enough to see the ultimate results. I am also sure that some who did survive long enough to see the results were shocked.

THE JUDGMENT OF HISTORY

I have been asked on occasion about what I think history will say of us who in recent years have been critical of an earlier generation of people involved with intellectual disabilities. I have come to believe that ultimately history will find us at fault for the way a very good idea, de-institutionalization, was carried out badly. I think we will be found wanting for the manner in which it was implemented. I think history will show that in many cases, it was a banner used for the political and economic abandonment of many people who continued to need our help. I think we will be found lacking in our vigilance over a process that needed to be watched very closely.

CHAPTER 10

John Lovelace and the Mercantile Theory of Mental Retardation

"DIAGNOSING MR. JEFFERSON"

For a number of years I have been intrigued by what might be termed the retrospective diagnosis of developmental disabilities. In my book *Minds Made Feeble: The Myth and Legacy of the Kallikaks,*[1] I expressed amazement that psychologist Henry Goddard in his study of the "good" and "bad" Kallikak families pronounced that a woman who had an illegitimate child in 1776 was "feebleminded." This was 136 years after the birth of the child. In fact, Goddard diagnosed entire generations of Kallikaks who neither he nor anyone alive at that time had ever seen, let alone tested with even the most crude of diagnostic techniques. Yet when his study was published in 1912, he asserted with confidence that he had found proof of a genetic basis for intellectual disabilities in these families.

Retrospective diagnosis by rumor or legend was common during the eugenics movement's zenith in the early 20th century. It continued as a practice in the United States and Europe until well after World War II.[2] Until recently, however, I mistakenly believed that retrospective diagnosis was now an historical artifact. I recognized how wrong I was when I happened on a book that proposed that a founding father belongs on the autism spectrum as well as on Mount Rushmore.

AUTISM AT MONTICELLO

In his book *Diagnosing Jefferson: Evidence of a Condition that Guided His Beliefs, Behavior, and Personal Associations,* Norm Ledgin speaks with certainty that Thomas Jefferson was a person with autism (more specifically, Asperger's Syndrome). Three attributes are presented to support his argument that Jefferson had this developmental disability. The first is the founding of the University of Virginia. Ledgin describes Jefferson's depth and intensity of involvement in designing the architecture, creating the curriculum, handpicking the faculty, prescribing student housing, and personally cataloguing the more than 6,000 books in the original library of the University. He actually refers to the University as "a tribute to his genius and I have no doubt a monument to obsessive behavior linked strongly to traits of Asperger's Syndrome."[3] He describes Jefferson's library cataloging as a savant-like trait reminiscent of those often attributed to people with autism.

The second characteristic of Jefferson described by Ledgin as being indicative of autism is his lack of money management skills. He states that Jefferson's inability to keep his income ahead of his debts is typical of Asperger's. He argues that this was " ... self-deluding ... [with Jefferson] believing somehow everything relating to money management would end well, [this] together with his keeping irreconcilable financial records—had evidently induced the situation."[4]

The third attribute that Ledgin discusses is perseveration. The evidence he presents for Jefferson's "belaboring a topic endlessly" is his letter writing. Ledgin points particularly to Jefferson's letters to Abigail Adams after a very intense political dispute with her husband, John Adams. His extensive correspondence with Abigail began when Jefferson's daughter Polly died, and it continued for years. After Jefferson and John Adams reconciled, they resumed direct correspondence. These later letters are described by Ledgin as "a treasure and a rich record of the outpourings of contrasting geniuses."[5] This is quite a different point of view from the "perseveration" he finds in Jefferson's earlier letters to Abigail.

Ledgin also ascribes several of Jefferson's personal relationship difficulties to autism. He argues that a lack of warmth toward his mother and Jefferson's reported inability to show affection to his own children are clearly indicative of Asperger's Syndrome.[6] Ledgin even makes a connection between Jefferson's affair with Sally Hemings and his claim that the third president had Asperger's. He writes that when he returned from France with Sally and having established a romantic relationship with her, "Jefferson faced the dilemma of balancing at home a private benefit that was taboo against his public image of propriety as a respecter of law and custom.[7] Explaining the connection, he goes on to say of people with Asperger's that they "live mentally and perhaps emotionally on two planes. They live in our world of nonautistics, but they carry with them a separate and otherworldly 'reality'—their reality . . . autistics seem to convert it [their reality] into something palpable."[8]

DISABILITIES AND "THE SAGE OF MONTICELLO"

I am unconvinced by Ledgin's arguments. I think his thesis that Jefferson had Asperger's is fraught with the same weakness and dangers that characterized the family pedigree studies of the eugenics movement. I appreciate the fact, however, that Ledgin's book led me to take another look at this remarkable individual and national icon.

Jefferson's actual experience with disability is documented in several sources. It was not the kind of personal experience portrayed by Ledgin; it was a familial experience. Thomas Jefferson was the sibling of a sister and a brother with disabilities. His relationships with them reveal much about his character as a brother and, perhaps, about the attitudes of his time and social class regarding disability.

Jefferson's younger sister Elizabeth has been characterized by a number of scholars as having had a serious and persisting disability.[9,10] She was described by one researcher with the words "rather deficient in intellect."[11] Jefferson cared for his sister after the death of their father. He administered his father's estate and saw to it that Elizabeth was attired and treated in a manner befitting a woman of the family's social status.[12]

Jefferson's account book records that on February 21, 1774, an intense nighttime earthquake forced all of the family to run outside their home at Monticello. Apparently frightened by the darkness and confusion, Elizabeth became separated from the rest of the family. She was found dead three days later, and on March 7 he recorded his sister's funeral in his account book.[13] In her biography of Jefferson, Fawn Brodie suggests that his feelings for Elizabeth might best be symbolized by a clipping in one of his scrapbooks. It is entitled "Elegy on the Death of an Idiot Girl" and it includes the line: "Poor guileless thing! . . . Heaven took thee spotless to his own."[14]

Jefferson's only brother, Randolph, has been described in Jefferson biographies as "retarded."[15] It is clear, however, that he lived a life that was characteristic of Southern planters in the 18th century. He married twice, had seven children, and lived on a large plantation.[16,17] On the other hand, he had limited verbal skills. His letters, many to his brother, are filled with grammatical errors, poor spelling, and scrawled handwriting. He was clearly no match for the famed intellect of his brother, Thomas. Still, there is no clear and convincing evidence of an intellectual disability. The evidence that does exist has led two researchers to state that "we might best say that Jefferson's brother would today be considered to have learning disabilities rather than mental retardation."[18]

While the nature of Randolph's disabilities can only be the subject of speculation at this point, it is clear that he experienced difficulties in several areas of his personal and vocational life, that he frequently called on his brother for assistance, and that he received the help he needed. Thomas advised Randolph on the running of his plantation and shared everything from dogs to vegetable seeds with him. He loaned him farming equipment and money and took his brother's beloved watch to Richmond for repair. He also wrote his brother's will for him.[19] In a deposition given in 1815, Thomas described his brother as "not possessing skill for the judicious management of his affairs." [20]

A man who lived as a slave at Monticello later dictated his memoirs of those years in 1847. Among the recollections of the man who was identified only as Isaac was a memory in which the former slave compares the intellect of Randolph Jefferson to his own in a self deprecating manner. Isaac said:

> Old Master's brother, Mass Randall, was a mighty simple man: used to come out among black people, play the fiddle and dance half the night; hadn't much more sense than Isaac.[21]

It may not be surprising that Isaac's comment has been used to claim that it was not Thomas but Randolph Jefferson who fathered Sally Hemings's children, and that Thomas was not involved sexually with her. In a book published by the Thomas Jefferson Heritage Society, the author writes that

> ... it should be noted that Randolph would be more likely to have a sexual encounter with Sally than would Thomas. Randolph was known to socialize with the black slaves at Monticello when he visited there ... And since Randolph was a widower at the time, it is easy to understand how he could become involved with one of the beautiful house servants ... In addition, Randolph was age 51 when Eston [a child claimed to be the son of Thomas Jefferson and Sally Hemings] was conceived while Thomas was 64. Randolph remarried a year after Eston was born, and fathered an additional son in that marriage, so he was evidently still sexually active throughout that time period.[22]

with him. He seemed to be a man who was knowledgeable about the business of running an adult home, but he also appeared to have a quiet respect for the consumers of his services. He truly seemed to like the men, and they seemed to like him.

FRONT PORCH INSIGHTS

While we sat on the porch I asked John for the first time about his family. Up to this point I had not begun to look into his background and knew little about his life before he came to the Burrell Home. I had to listen closely to his comments about his early life because, as I have said earlier, I had difficulty at times understanding his speech. I frequently asked him to repeat himself or to speak more loudly. I know this became annoying to him after a while, but he persisted in trying to tell me his story. He told me first that his mother had been shot by a little boy who was cleaning a gun (a 22 rifle, he said). John said that he was just a child when this happened to his mother. This part of his story proved to be accurate when I had the chance to trace his life history. I became confused, however, when John went on to say that his mother was killed by a car. Of course later I understood that this was his memory of the death of his foster mother, Mrs. Hunter. He also told me that his father's name was John Lovelace, "same as mine." This was actually his grandfather. His father was never identified in the community and only once in the hospital records of his mother. I decided later that it would serve no purpose to discuss that name with him. My conversation with John that afternoon made me even more convinced that his abilities had been underestimated over the years. It also made me more sensitive to how frustrating it must have been throughout most of his life for John to have such difficulty making himself understood to others.

VISITS TO THE MINI-MART

Twice each day Bob Williams took a van load of men to a mini-mart a few miles from the Little Ponderosa. On one of my visits I went along with John for a trip to the store. The men rode quietly to the market and did not have much to say while they did their shopping. Their actions while in the store, however, were very deliberate and focused. The owner of the mini-mart seemed very receptive to the men as they entered. Apparently he had come to expect their visits and appreciated their business. As soon as the men entered the store they walked with great intention to the coffee pots, the soft drink coolers, and the snack shelves. They quickly took their selections to the counter and asked for packs of cigarettes to add to their purchases. One man even asked for a carton of Winstons, obviously his regular brand.

John had only a small amount of change with him. I told him that I wanted to treat him to something and asked what he would like. His reply was no surprise to me. He wanted a large cup of coffee and some cigarettes. While he poured his coffee, I paid for it and for several packs of cigarettes. I did this with mixed feelings. As a reformed smoker, I always felt a twinge of guilt at buying something for John which I knew could do him harm. On the other hand, again as a former smoker, I understood his addiction. I also understood that smoking was one of the few pleasures that he had in his life. And so, my buying cigarettes for him became a part of our relationship. Although I tried to vary the kinds of gifts I gave him for birthdays, Christmas, and other occasions, I knew that it was cigarettes and cigarette money that he most appreciated and, in fact, needed.

What became most clear to me from this visit to the mini-mart with John and the other men was the difference between the discretionary resources available to the others and the money that John had for his personal use. John had a monthly allowance of $30 for all of his personal expenses. This money had to cover everything other than his room and board, and whatever other maintenance and care might be provided by the adult home. The combined funding from Social Security disability benefits and Virginia supplementary benefits for his care came to $521 per month. This amount was paid directly to the Little Ponderosa, just as it had been earlier to Burrell Home. This was the standard amount of funding for adult home care for people with disabilities with no income or other resources available to them. This translated into approximately $17 per day for his housing, food, care, recreation, and a profit for the adult home operator. Obviously the profit margin could only be increased by economizing as far as possible with the expenses for housing, food, and staffing. I saw less evidence of this cost cutting at the Little Ponderosa than I had seen elsewhere. This may have been at least partially due to the greater funding for services provided to the veterans who lived there.

I do not know how much personal money the Veterans Administration provided the veterans at the Little Ponderosa; I was told it varied with the degree of disability and other factors that became part of a formula for determining benefits. I am sure that many of these men also received money from their families or from other sources. I do know, however, that the resources they had stood in dramatic contrast to John's $30 a month. From this amount it was expected that he would buy his toiletries, clothing, entertainment, refreshments, and anything else he might need. Obviously in John's case almost every penny of it went for cigarettes and, even at that, it was not enough to keep him supplied all month. It was not nearly enough!

The next few months seemed to go fairly smoothly for John at the Little Ponderosa. It appeared that he was getting along well with the other residents. He was working several days each week at a nearby sheltered workshop. This seemed to be particularly important to him because through his work there he was able to earn extra money, which helped with his cigarette needs.

It was during this time that I asked John to sign release forms so that I could look at his records at the Central Virginia Training Center and at his Department of Social Service records since his discharge. I also made several trips to the town where he had grown up to check on courthouse records and old newspapers in the public library. All of this information came together in a way that allowed me to understand more fully John's life history.

During these months I also visited John several times at the Little Ponderosa. I usually walked around the grounds a bit with him, talked with Bob Williams about how things were going, and took John for a shopping trip to the mini-mart. One time I took him a cardboard trunk full of some clothing that I could no longer wear but that I thought would fit him. I also thought that we wore the same size shoes, and I took him several pairs. I thought the trunk would fit under his bed. It didn't, and soon it was crushed from the bumpings it got at the foot of his bed. Most of the clothing didn't fit or wasn't appropriate for the kind of laundering done at the Ponderosa. The shoes were too tight, and I found out later that one particularly nice pair had been traded for a pack of cigarettes.

TROUBLE ON TINKER MOUNTAIN

During one of these visits Bob Williams told me that there had been complaints from the sheltered workshop that John was coming to work with torn clothing and body odor. He explained that it simply wasn't possible for the adult home to provide deodorant and new clothing. Bob had given John a pair of his own used running shoes, and I know that John wore these regularly for many months. It all came back, however, to the same bind. John only had $30 each month, all of that went for cigarettes. He was earning a little extra money now at the workshop, but they wanted him to spend more on clothing and personal hygiene. The more familiar you become with how the system works for many poor people and many with disabilities, the more it begins to appear to be filled with "Catch 22s." I bought John some deodorant, and we scratched together some better clothing. John and I also talked about the importance of his meeting the expectations and standards of the workshop so that he could continue working there. I hoped for the best.

On July 19, 1988, I received a call from Bob Williams. John had been sent home from the workshop in late June because of a temper tantrum. He would not be allowed to return. I talked with John a few days later and he pleaded with me to help him get his job back. He was very upset that he would no longer have a way to make extra money. He was unable to really explain what had happened when he was terminated but assured me that if he had another chance he would control his behavior. I wrote to the director of the workshop and asked about the incident that led to John's termination. I tried to frame my inquiry with fairness to the people at the workshop whom I was certain had made a difficult decision in John's case. I hope that excerpts from my letter are indicative of that attempt at fairness:

> ...I talked with Mr. Bob Williams of Little Ponderosa recently concerning John Lovelace. He explained that John was terminated from involvement at Tinker Mountain Industries in late June. It is my understanding that John was terminated because of a temper tantrum, and consequent aggressive and hostile behavior.
>
> I have known John Lovelace for about a year and a half. During that time I have come to feel a responsibility to him as a friend/advocate. I would appreciate any further description you could give me concerning the circumstances of John's separation from Tinker Mountain.
>
> Please understand that I am not questioning the action which has been taken, I simply need to have a better insight on what is happening in John's life at this time. I am on the Board of Directors of Lynchburg Sheltered Industries and I fully comprehend that difficult decisions must be made about individuals in light of the best interests of the overall organization.
>
> Thank you for your assistance with this matter. I hope you are having a pleasant summer...

I received a courteous letter from the sheltered workshop indicating their willingness to help me understand better the circumstances of John's termination there. They required that I have John sign a release form before they would share with me any information. I had become accustomed to this requirement by then and did the necessary paperwork. It did take time, however, for everything to be processed and it was early August before I knew the exact circumstances of John's dismissal from the workshop. I received a long letter of explanation from the woman who had followed John's case most closely there. Her report included the following:

> . . . John began his latest employment with Tinker Mountain Industries on March 22, 1988. The agreement was that John was to work two days a week . . . John did not keep to the agreement and began coming every day. When he was here every day, John was often verbally abusive to staff as well as his coworkers. I discussed the behaviors with John on several occasions. He agreed that he would try to do better.
>
> (On) April 21, 1988, Mr. Williams from Little Ponderosa telephoned me about John's behavior at home. We agreed that five days a week for John seemed to be too much. After much discussion with John and Mr. Williams, John agreed to work on Mondays, Tuesdays, and Fridays beginning April 26, 1988. During this time John's behavior became worse. He was grouchy and looked tired. He asked about returning to work five days a week whenever he was here. John did not understand that we were concerned about his health and his well-being. John said that he wanted to work in order to obtain more money.
>
> A minor problem with John was that he often had bad body odor. John was informed that in order to keep working at TMI he must bathe and wear appropriate clothing to work. A telephone call was made to Little Ponderosa stating the same. John's clothing was often torn and dirty.
>
> On June 20, 1988, John came to me asking that he be allowed to work five days a week. I explained that his behavior on this day had been unacceptable. He had already yelled at his supervisor for not being able to bring him more work right away. Later in the afternoon, John yelled at his coworker for not bringing him work. [John was doing piece work. The more items he completed each day the more he earned. He was probably very sensitive to the importance of always having a supply of work to do available to him at his table.] He proceeded to throw a box of work on the floor. When counseled about his behavior, John stated that he couldn't make any money working three days a week. He apologized for his previous behavior and said that he would try not to be angry but talk with his case manager instead.
>
> Approximately five minutes later, John literally threw work at another employee. He balled up his fist to hit him. If I had not told John at that point not to, he would have hit him. John was asked to come to my office to calm down. He threw his glasses on the floor. Another case manager picked up his glasses for him. John got out of the chair and hit the wall as he walked out of the room.
>
> It was at this point that TMI staff called Little Ponderosa. We asked that someone pick him up immediately. John was asked to stay in the cafeteria. John threw a chair and he attempted to push over a floor fan. John was then asked to go outside. We felt that if he smoked a cigarette he

would feel better. Once outside John calmed down some. He said that he had to work five days a week. The rehabilitation manager and I explained that we were concerned about his health and behaviors such as those he had exhibited on this day. It was explained to John that he was suspended from work for two days. He was told there was a possibility of termination.

... [a] meeting was held to discuss John's case. It was the decision of the group that he would be terminated due to poor health and aggressive behaviors toward clients as well as staff.

Professor Smith, I have tried to enclose all of the particulars of John's separation from TMI. Please notify me if there is other information needed. I have also enclosed several incident reports and a progress report for your information.

The incident reports documented what the letter indicated. John had repeatedly lashed out at others at the workshop. His anger exploded when he felt that his "livelihood" was in jeopardy. He wanted to work five days a week in order to have more income. The income was critical to him but his attempts at protecting it only resulted in losses.

SURPLUS PEOPLE

I wrote back to the workshop expressing my understanding of their actions. Indeed, John had become a threat to the well-being of the staff and other clients there. They had given him repeated chances to redeem himself, but he was unable to do so. I once read a spoof in a professional journal on some of the exotic theories of mental retardation that have been developed over the years. As part of this satire a fictitious person was described as having developed the mercantile theory of mental retardation. It went into considerable detail in giving a burlesque portrayal of the theory. After having come to understand some of the dilemmas in John's life, however, I find some truth in this satire. Indeed, his life had been most handicapped by his inability to find the resources he needed in order to effectively trade or exchange with others to meet his own needs. His frustrations and difficulties had, more often than not, centered on his lack of the capacity to be productive and earn his own way to the goals he had for himself. I expect that this is a common experience for many others labeled with intellectual disabilities. Being mentally retarded in this sense comes down to not being a part of the economic and social system. It is being outside of the commerce of life and, therefore, having no value to that system. It is the experience of being a surplus person. This is the experience that many people with intellectual disabilities share with others who because of age, background, or other disability are viewed as having no value.

Perhaps the issue of human rights and the practices of sterilization, institutionalization, and other forms of exclusion of people with intellectual disabilities was put into its unfortunate context most poignantly by John H. Bell, the former superintendent of the Lynchburg institution where John was confined for most of his adult life and the successful defendant in the *Buck v. Bell* sterilization decision of 1927. In speaking of people classified as feebleminded he said, "there was never a more fallacious statement than that all men are born free and equal."[25] It is ironic that the Lynchburg State Colony, where Dr. Bell was superintendent, was located only 60 miles from Monticello, the home of the author of the Declaration of Independence.

CHAPTER 11

Darwin's Last Child
Disability, Family, and Friends

The term *eugenics,* derived from the Greek word eugenes meaning well-born, was first used by Francis Galton in 1883 to describe what he envisioned as a new discipline. He defined *eugenics* as a science through which the influences that could improve the inborn qualities of races and classes of human beings could be discovered. One of the primary aims of eugenicists was the elimination from human populations of unwanted hereditary disorders through the use of selective marriage practices. Quickly, however, and as discussed earlier, the movement also embraced the promotion of compulsory sterilization of people with traits that were judged to be undesirable, institutionalization of people diagnosed as defective, and restrictions on the immigration of people whose race or nationality was deemed to possess inferior hereditary qualities.

Galton was a cousin of Charles Darwin. It is not surprising, therefore, that the concepts and language of the theory of evolution were associated with eugenics from its inception. The discourse on social policy regarding mental retardation and other disabilities in the late nineteenth century and early twentieth century was filled with references to the survival of the fittest and the struggle for existence. Eugenics was presented as applied science founded on the central biological theory of evolution. Eugenicists were obsessed with the elimination of people who were considered defective, and they viewed public policy that promoted the welfare of people with disabilities as an interference with the process of natural selection.

Darwin made references to intellectual disabilities in his major work on human evolution, *The Descent of Man*. He compared what he observed to be the imitative behavior of people with mental retardation, to our "nearest allies, the monkeys," and the "barbarous races of mankind." Darwin drew other parallels between the behavior of people with mental retardation and animals. He described them as smelling their food like animals before eating it and cited a reference to an "idiot . . . smelling every mouthful of food before eating it."[1] Darwin closed his discussion by describing people with mental retardation as having filthy habits, no sense of decency and, like animals, having remarkably hairy bodies.

Darwin conceived of people with intellectual disabilities as evolutionary mistakes. He speculated that retardation resulted from reversions in the developmental process. From his perspective, persons with mental retardation displayed the characteristics of other species and what he considered to be inferior races of human beings. They had reverted to these life forms even though they were born to parents of a superior level of evolutionary development. For reasons that were not clear to him, something had caused an error in reproduction that resulted in an individual who looked and behaved like a member of an inferior group or species.

A similar concept was developed by J. Langdon Down in his theory of the racial nature of mental retardation. Darwin's influence is very evident in Down's observations on what was to become known as Down syndrome. He termed it *mongolian idiocy*. In his essay, "Observations on an Ethnic Classification of Idiots," Down described children and adults that he thought were the products of "degeneracy." Although he provided little detail on the mechanisms of this phenomenon, Down theorized that in the case of "mongolism" the evolutionary degeneracy was caused most often by "tuberculosis in the parents."[2]

Charles Darwin became an icon for scientific explanations of both biological and social phenomena. Thus, his impact on scientific and public perceptions of disability has been enormous. The theory of evolution, as interpreted through social Darwinism, had tremendous consequences for hundreds of thousands of people. Arguments concerning the meaning of disability, and the political and economic responses to that meaning, are still influenced by Darwin's observations and their derivatives.

There is, however, another facet to what we know about Darwin's understanding of the human issues associated with disability. Through his relationship with his youngest child, his youngest son who had an intellectual disability, we are able to see a different and contradictory view. Through the prism of Darwin's personal experience, this giant of the scientific world viewed disability in a different light.

Lewis Thomas, in his book *The Medusa and the Snail*, expressed misgivings about a total reliance on science for knowledge. He explained, "The only solid piece of scientific truth about which I am totally confident is that we are profoundly ignorant about nature."[3] Michael Merleau-Ponty also commented on expanding our vision of knowledge:

> I cannot shut myself up within the realm of science. All my knowledge of the world, even scientific knowledge, is gained from my own particular point of view, or from some experience of the world . . . The whole universe of science is built upon the world as directly experienced . . . we must begin by reawakening the basic experience of the world.

At the time that Darwin was working on *The Origin of Species*, the book that would establish his place in the history of science, he was also worried about the health of his children. He had been preoccupied with his own health throughout his life and feared that his marriage to his cousin, Emma Edgewood, placed their children at special risk for "hereditary ill-health." Indeed, several of their children did suffer with chronic illnesses. Darwin was deeply and continually concerned for his ailing children and for the illnesses that Emma experienced. One of the most agonizing aspects of his family life, however, came with the birth of his last child, Charles Waring Darwin, who was his namesake.[4] Emma conceived this child when she was 48 years old. She was apparently quite uncomfortable and uneasy during the pregnancy. A description of her discomfort, and a comment about the new baby and his fate, was recorded by Darwin's daughter Henrietta:

> This had been a suffering year for my mother. Her last child, Charles Waring Darwin, was born on December 6th, 1856. I remember very well the weary months she passed, and reading aloud to her sometimes to help her bear her discomforts. The poor little baby was born without its full share of intelligence. Both my mother and father were infinitely tender towards him but, when he died in the summer of 1858, after their first sorrow, they could only feel thankful. He had never learnt [sic] to walk or talk.[5]

The baby's disability was apparently noticed quickly by the Darwins. Although there is no documentation that sufficiently describes the nature of the child's intellectual disability, it has been speculated, largely on the basis of Emma's age, that Charles Waring had Down syndrome. Regardless of diagnosis and cause, however, Darwin wrote a sensitive and detailed description of his son as a memorial to him following his death. His words reveal his deep love of the child and elucidate the impressions of his daughter Henrietta:

> Our poor baby was born December 6th, 1856 and died on June 28th, 1858, and was therefore above 18 months old. He was small for his age and backward in walking and talking, but intelligent and observant. When crawling naked on the floor he looked very elegant. He had never been ill and cried less than any of our babies. He was of a remarkably sweet, placid and joyful disposition; but had not high spirits, and did not laugh much. He often made strange grimaces and shivered, when excited; but did so also, for a joke and his little eyes used to glisten, after pouting out or stretching widely his little lips. He used sometimes to move his mouth as if talking loudly, but making no noise, and this he did when very happy. He was particularly fond of standing on one of my hands and being tossed in the air; and then he always smiled, and made a little pleased noise. I had just taught him to kiss me with open mouth, when I told him. He would lie for a long time placidly on my lap looking with a steady and pleased expression at my face; sometimes trying to poke his poor little fingers into my mouth, or making nice little bubbling noises as I moved his chin. I had taught him not to scratch, but when I said, "Giddlums never scratches now" he could not always resist a little grab, and then he would look at me with a wicked little smile. He would play for any length of time on the sofa, letting himself fall suddenly, and looking over his shoulder to see that I was ready. He was very affectionate and had a passion for Parslow [the Darwin's butler] and it was very pretty to see his extreme eagerness with outstretched arms, to get to him. Our poor little darling's short life has been placid, innocent and joyful. I think and trust he did not suffer so much at last, as he appeared to do; but the last 36 hours were miserable beyond expression. In the sleep of Death he resumed his placid looks. [6]

These beautiful and caring words of a father for his lost child are a testament to the value of a child with a disability to his family. They are the most poignant and moving expressions that I have read from this genius of modern science. They remind me of the contributions that people with disabilities often make to their parents, siblings, and communities. The words stand in stark contrast to Darwin's description of the similarities of persons with mental retardation to animals. They provide an important glimpse of the human side of our knowledge of what disabilities are and how they should be constructed for others to understand. His words remind us that social definitions and roles are created by the personal meaning we have for one another.

Simi Linton issued a call for conceptualizing disabilities in a way that more completely recognizes the natural spectrum of human diversity. To achieve a full appreciation of the complementarity and interdependence of people, the eyes of both science and passion are required. Commenting on the work of Nobel laureate and geneticist, Barbara McClintock, Linton wrote, "If something doesn't fit there's a reason, and you find what it is. Rather than overlook difference, for instance, by naming an exception an aberration, a contaminant, she worked to understand its place and function."[7] It appears that Darwin's last son taught him in a personal sense that intellectual disability was not an aberration or a contaminant.

In his book *Awakenings,* Oliver Sacks wrote about a question he once asked A. R. Luria. When Sacks asked him what he considered to be the most interesting thing in the world, Luria replied, "I cannot express it in one word, I have to use two. I would have to speak of a 'romantic science.' It has been my life's hope to found or refound a romantic science."[8] In recent years some critics of the effort to redefine and reconceptualize disabilities have called for a dichotomous separation between a scientific understanding of disabilities and the romance of disability advocacy and activism. On the contrary, it seems to me, it is crucial to the lives of millions of people that we create a "romantic science" of disability.

HOMETOWN FRIENDS

The summer of 1988 was long and frustrating for John. He was no longer working at the workshop and he had little to do with his time. In addition, his glasses were broken. They had survived the toss he gave them in anger at the workshop, but the frames were broken when he accidently sat on them on his bed at the Little Ponderosa one morning. After the frames were broken a lens was misplaced. I had a call from Bob Williams explaining the situation. It would be possible for John to get replacements through the Community Services Board in Roanoke, but the wait would probably be several months. Bob also reported that John behaved as if he were blind without his glasses. He literally needed to be guided from place to place. This was my first true awareness of how limited John's vision had become.

I told Bob I would give the matter some thought, and that I would be back to him soon. I was troubled at the thought of how disabled John was without his glasses and the long delay there would be in getting him help through the state system. I was so frustrated that I almost called Bob back immediately to tell him to schedule an appointment for John at my expense. I had no idea what the cost would be but guessed that the lenses he needed would be expensive. One other possibility occurred to me, however, before I made the call back to Bob. My friend Bill Hadden was very active at the national level with the Lion's Club. Bill, who is blind himself, is also very active with Leader Dogs for the Blind. I knew that sight conservation and services to blind people have long been projects of the Lion's Club. I gave Bill a call and explained the situation to him. Before I hung up I had his assurance that the Lions would pay for both the examination and the glasses. He gave me an address for the billing of the charges. Soon John had new glasses. I am still very grateful to Bill Hadden and to the Lions of Virginia.

During this time I contacted the Department of Social Services in Martinsville, the town where John was born and grew up. It was there also that he was originally placed when he was de-institutionalized from the Central Virginia Training Center. I asked for their help in allowing me to review John's records that were in their files. Of course this meant another round of the release forms to which I had become so accustomed. This had become routine for me, and soon I had completed everything which was necessary for access to John's folder.

These records showed that John's "freedom" in the adult home to which he was initially discharged from the Lynchburg institution lasted less than a year. After the fight he had with another resident who lost two teeth in the confrontation, John was removed briefly, as discussed earlier, and then returned to the home. Before the year was up, however, he had been in other trouble and was sent to another facility. This was a larger home. John lived there for two years and was employed at a workshop nearby. He was "fired" from the workshop and discharged from the home within two years. He was then sent to an adult home in Roanoke. He lived there for two years and worked at Tinker Mountain Industries. He was then transferred to another adult home in Roanoke where he lived for less than a year. Finally, he found himself at Burrell Home. His residency there would last less than two years, and the events that brought John to my attention would occur during this time. In addition to these records, there was a curious entry in his folder which indicated that a call had been made to Social Services in Martinsville about the time of the no-code order at Burrell, which informed the people there that he had a brain tumor and was not expected to live. I interpreted this anticipation to be another indication of the degree to which he had been written off as a lost person.

While I was visiting in Martinsville I became acquainted with a social worker who had been responsible in part for processing the forms that were necessary for John's disability benefits to be paid to the various adult homes where he had lived since leaving the Central Virginia Training Center. John was largely just a name to her. She had never met him but was, of course, aware of his frequent moves and the reasons for his transfers. I talked with her at length on two occasions. She proved to be a very compassionate person, and she was interested in John's story. I shared with her most of what I have included so far in this book. She was intrigued and moved by the plight of the human being she had known only as a name, and a problem. She had lots of questions about his current living situation at the Little Ponderosa, and she seemed genuinely glad that life was somewhat better for him there.

Two days before Christmas in 1988 I visited John to deliver a card and small gift. My wife had also prepared something special for him to eat. We talked and he opened his gift. Then he was quite anxious to show me something that he had gotten from his "hometown." A large box had arrived the day before with a tag that read, "From your friends in Martinsville." The package was neatly packed and the wrapping that it came in was beautiful. There was a nice card inside that was signed only, again, as from "friends." The gifts in the box included some nice used clothing (a jacket, two sweaters, and several pairs of pants), new clothing (several pairs of underwear and socks), deodorant and other toiletries, and a large can of roasted peanuts. John was obviously moved by the gift and was especially touched that it came from people in his "hometown" of Martinsville.

HIDING COMPASSION

Knowing, of course, that the gifts had come from the social worker in Martinsville, I wrote to her on Christmas day and thanked her for John, and for me, for the special joy that she had brought to this holiday. She truly had, I thought, brought the spirit of Christmas alive with her caring expression of charity and concern. When I saw her several weeks later she thanked me but then took me aside. She asked that I not mention to anyone that she had sent the gifts. She explained that one of the reasons that she had signed the card and tag as "friends" was that agency regulations prohibited employees from becoming "personally involved" with clients. She was afraid that if her gifts to John became known she could be found in violation of agency rules! I assured her that I would protect her anonymity. How very sad it is when caring and compassion become violations of bureaucratic procedure. I have found it true, however, that more and more professionals in what used to be called the "caring" professions now find that they are in "human service" work that is narrowly defined and where signs of emotional involvement with those they "serve" are viewed either as embarrassments or breaches of policy.

THE FIRING OF THE "NIGHT MAN"

Bob Williams called me on January 24 to tell me that he had fired the "night man" at the Little Ponderosa. This was the man who came in at 11 o'clock each night and stayed until seven in the morning. He was alone with the residents during this time, but most of the men went to bed early after watching television and didn't usually get up until it was nearly time for him to leave. He was essentially a night watchman who did a bit of cleaning during his shift. His only contact with the men otherwise was when they would awaken and go to the lounge for a smoke. This happened frequently but usually lasted only long enough for a single cigarette. Occasionally more than one man would wake for a smoke at the same time.

Bob explained to me that he had fired the night man because John complained that the man had kicked him. After investigating this a bit Bob found that this was true. John had a cut and a bruise, and another man had witnessed the kick. Bob said that there was some confusion concerning the circumstances. He said that the night man claimed John went into a shouting tantrum when he would not give him a cigarette. Bob said, however, that regardless of the circumstances the man had violated the Ponderosa's standards by reacting to John with physical force. Bob repeated to me several times his apology for the man's actions, and his concern that I know right away what had happened. I thanked him for his thoughtfulness and our call ended. I was left at the end of our conversation, however, with the sad sense that things were beginning to fall apart again in John's life.

MAKING ANOTHER MOVE

In less than a week I had another call from Bob Williams. John had continued to have temper outbursts. When he attempted to talk with

John about these episodes he could get little out of him except that he wanted to go back to work. Bob said that he had talked with the case manager at the Roanoke Community Services Board office and, in his words, John had been "written off when it comes to work, there is no chance." Bob told me that he did not think that he could continue to have John live at the Little Ponderosa. He felt that John's disability and life situation was so different from the other men there that it simply wasn't going to work.

Bob did have a suggestion to make about a different living arrangement for John. He explained that he was the part owner of another adult home. This one was located in a little village about 50 miles west of Roanoke. It was called the Draper Valley Rest Home. He described the facility to me and explained that more of the residents there were people with intellectual disabilities. He also said that the community services case managers there had been very helpful in arranging employment for the residents at a sheltered workshop nearby. He assured me that the facility was actually nicer than the Little Ponderosa and that John would have a semi-private room there instead of the bunk style arrangement he had currently. Bob seemed to be seeking my blessing for switching John to Draper Valley. He was very positive in his conversation with me, but it was also obvious that the end of John's time at the Little Ponderosa had come, and the alternative that Bob was offering was the only one readily available. For what it was worth, I gave my "blessing." Within days the appropriate social service agency documents had been executed, and John was on his way to Draper Valley Rest Home.

Soon after John's move, and before I had a chance to visit with him in his new home, I wrote to the administrator of Draper Valley. Her name was Frances Martin, and she was spoken of very highly by Bob Williams. He said that he had explained to her my interest in John. I hoped that my letter to her would reinforce the idea that John had someone "on the outside" who was keeping track of his life. My letter to her included the following:

> I am a friend and advocate for John Lovelace. Bob Williams may have mentioned that I try to watch out for John's best interests. I hope that he is doing well in his new home. I also hope that by now John has been able to start to work at the sheltered workshop. I know that he will be much happier being able to work each day. I understand that there will also be recreational programs available for John. Please read this letter to him after you finish with it and give it to him to keep. John, I hope that you like your new home. It sounds very nice. I look forward to seeing

you at Camp Virginia Jaycee on March 31. Bob Williams should be getting the information about the camp weekend soon. I hope you have started working or will real soon. Please remember the importance of getting along with everyone there as best as you can. I am hoping that you will be very happy living in Draper.

Take care. I will see you soon.

Sincerely,

Dave

On the same day that I wrote this letter I also wrote to the head of the Mormon Church in Lynchburg whom I had met some years before. Mrs. Hunter, John's foster mother, had been a member of the Mormon Church and had taken him to church regularly. Some of his old records at the Lynchburg Training School and Hospital had listed his religion as being Mormon. I had contacted the church leader earlier explaining some things about John's life and current circumstances, and asking that the Mormon congregation in Roanoke be informed about John. I hoped that they would visit with him and take an interest. My thinking was that John needed as many ties as possible in the community, and that this might further reduce his loneliness. Representatives of the Mormon Church in Roanoke had, indeed, visited him, read to him, and brought him presents.

This letter explained his move and appealed for continued contact:

Thank you so much for your help with John Lovelace. Members of the Mormon Church visited with him at the Little Ponderosa, and I know it meant a great deal to him to have this contact with the Church he grew up with in Martinsville.

There is, however, a bit of a complication to the contact established with John. He is now living in a different facility. He was recently moved to the Draper Valley Rest Home near Radford. The living arrangement there is better for John and there is a sheltered workshop nearby where he will be able to work each day.

I know that John would appreciate having visitors from the Mormon Church visit him in his new home. Would you please arrange for a congregation near Blacksburg or Radford to make contact with him?

I gave him John's address and thanked him again for his help. I also wrote a note that same day to the social worker in Martinsville drawing her attention to John's move. I assumed that she might have seen or executed some of the paperwork involved, and I encouraged her continued personal, but anonymous, interest in John. I hoped that his "friends" in Martinsville would continue to remember him at special times.

SEEKING NEW FRIENDS

It was around this same time that I made another decision which was aimed at connecting John in various ways to communities that might help, encourage, or protect him. I have mentioned earlier the work of Mike Hudson. Mike had been working for many months on a series of articles about adult homes for the *Roanoke Times and World-News*. I had come to know of his research and the planned series through my friend Mary Bishop, another writer for the newspaper. Mary is a brilliant and compassionate reporter who was a finalist for a Pulitzer Prize in 1989 for her series on corruption and unsafe practices in the home pests extermination industry. We had shared an earlier interest in the issue of involuntary sexual sterilization. She had written two newspaper stories about a woman named Sallie Wilcher who was needlessly institutionalized and sterilized in 1929. When Sallie was institutionalized her two-year-old son was taken from her. Nearly 60 years later, after no idea of where her son was, Mary helped Sallie locate the son's wife. Her son was deceased but Sallie at least had the opportunity of learning about his life and about her grandchildren. Unfortunately, she died before meeting them.

I had asked for Mary's advice on several occasions as I tried to find ways to be a friend to John. It occurred to me after a while that if John's story were made public in some way that two things might result. One, if the no-code incident was made public it might help insure that it would never occur again in John's life. Two, it might make others less vulnerable to the same thing. Finally, I thought that if a newspaper account of John's life were published there was a chance that someone or some organization might take an interest in him and provide him with some level of support.

Quite frankly, I invited Mary to lunch one day and asked her to look over the material that I had gathered from the Lynchburg Training School records, and the other sources, and to see if she would be willing to write John's story for the newspaper. She promised to give it serious consideration.

When I next heard from Mary she suggested that we meet with Mike Hudson and the editor that both of them worked with, a man named Rich Martin. She explained that she really felt that John's story belonged with Mike's series on adult homes. She felt that in this context it would be better understood and that it would receive more attention. She had also been impressed with the thoroughness and care Mike was giving to the series. She was confident that he would be just as conscientious about John's story. Mary knew that I was still having some anxiety about making John's story public. Her reassurance was helpful to me.

When we met with Mike and Rich they explained that John's story would follow two or three days of major articles on adult homes and the people who live in them. They were excited about the human face that John's life story would bring to the series. As the meeting progressed I became more confident that the story would be in good hands. Although I could not ask for editing privileges, of course, Mike offered to let me read a draft of the story before it was published. He also asked if we could visit John together before he wrote the story. We left with a tentative understanding that Mike could do the story, but I did ask that I have the chance to talk with John before it proceeded further. I talked with him later that week and explained the idea of the newspaper story as best I could. He readily agreed, but once again I think that he agreed out of friendship rather than out of a deep grasp of the significance of the story. I called Mike and told him that he could write the story, and we also arranged to visit John together. John's story was published in the *Roanoke Times and World-News* on October 5, 1989. It was a front-page story with a large color photograph of John sitting on his bed at the Draper Valley Rest Home. The story opened with a description of John's birth and early life in Martinsville. A detailed description of his life at the Lynchburg Training School and Hospital followed, and then came a discussion of his de-institutionalization after 20 years there.

Mike's article continued with an account of his years in Lynchburg Training School and Hospital and the circumstances of his discharge. It gave a listing of the homes that he had lived in since he was de-institutionalized, and the unfortunate circumstances that had led to his leaving each of them. It followed his life up to the point of his departure from the Little Ponderosa. Finally, it concluded with a description of his life situation at the time the article was published. It was a thorough and moving account of John's life. I hoped it would elicit concern and support by some of the readers of the piece. I was mistaken.

CHAPTER 12

"Fairview Is Nice to Me"

THE ARAYAN NATIONS, A CLEFT PALATE, AND EPIPHANY

In 1992, Floyd Cochran was the chief recruiter for the Aryan Nations. As the fifth-ranking leader of this self-proclaimed Nazi/white supremacist organization, he was admired for his skill in dealing effectively with the public and a critical press. Cochran was also very successful in using his media savvy and marketing skills to attract young people to the organization. He became the group's national spokesman and was described by the Aryan Nations' chief, the Reverend Richard Butler, as being destined to be "the next Goebbels."[1] In July of that year, however, Floyd Cochran was suddenly ordered off the Nation's compound. The Reverend Butler gave him five minutes to leave.

The rift in Cochran's relationship with the Arayan Nations had begun earlier that year. Shortly before he was to speak at the Hitler Youth Festival in Idaho, Cochran mentioned to the Nations' security chief that he was running late because he had been on the telephone with his wife. He was very concerned about his four-year-old son, who was having surgery to correct a cleft palate. The chief's response to Cochran was, "He's a genetic defect. When we come to power, he'll have to be euthanized."[2]

Cochran reported later that he was stunned by this remark. He had studied Ku Klux Klan and Nazi literature for almost 25 years. Until that moment, however, he had not faced a sobering fact. The intolerance for human differences he had preached for decades was now being applied to someone he loved. When he voiced his concern over this issue, he was given the order to leave the Arayan Nations' property immediately.

Floyd Cochran soon began to speak and write about the hateful philosophy and practices of the Aryan Nations. His son's disability and Richard Butler's attitude toward it had changed his life.

THE THAWING OF A SOUL

Eldridge Cleaver, the author of the startling book on race and racism, *Soul on Ice,* died in May 1998. During the 1960s and 1970s he was known as a fiery and eloquent voice for the Black Power movement. After writing his book in prison, he became known as one of the infamous organizers of the Black Panther Party in 1966, along with Huey Newton and Bobby Seale.

In 1968, while serving as information officer for the Black Panthers, Cleaver was involved in a shoot-out with police in Oakland, California. Wounded in the gun battle, he was arrested. He later jumped bail and fled to Algeria. Cleaver returned to the United States in 1975. After a long legal battle he was convicted of assault, placed on probation, and required to do public service.

In *Soul on Ice,* Cleaver spoke with rage of the experiences of African Americans and with angry disbelief of the oblivious attitudes of most white people regarding their own racism. It is rare to find a line in the book that does not scream with bitterness. Yet, Cleaver closes one of his chapters with these words: "The price of hating other human beings is loving oneself less."[3]

During the years following his return to the United States, Eldridge Cleaver was not visible as a public figure. He was no longer regarded as a symbol of race pride and race rage. Cleaver's historic identity, however, continued to be that of a figure associated with a separatist philosophy and a militant strategy toward race relations. Given that persona, it is interesting to consider some of the public remarks he made in the early 1990s about his youngest child, Riley. Cleaver made these statements after he became an activist and advocate for children and adults with disabilities. Riley was born with Down syndrome.

In a 1993 speech, Cleaver described his feelings when he learned that his expected son had proven to be positive for Down syndrome through an amniocentesis test. He spoke candidly of his lack of understanding of the implications of the test and his absence of sensitivity to the humanity and needs of the child who was to come into his life. He admitted, in fact, that he was only following the lead of his child's mother in accepting and preparing for Riley.

With Riley's birth came the barrage of terms and decisions that often engulf parents of children with disabilities. Cleaver found that the birth of his son coincided with a period when he was questioning himself about his own future. He was no longer a leader of the Black Panther Party and he did not see a role for himself in the civil rights movement in the 1990s. With the birth of a child with Down syndrome, however, Cleaver found that "I no longer had to wonder what I was going to do, I was doing it. I had my hands full . . . It was a struggle to understand and comprehend the situation itself, and it was a shock and a struggle to begin to realize that I was involved in a very hostile environment. I began to meet other parents . . . We began to realize that we were up against the school system, and the legal system, and the medical system."[4]

As Cleaver described his feelings of being "up against" the various social systems of his culture as his son's advocate, his words became reminiscent of the anger he expressed concerning American racism in *Soul on Ice.* Through his struggle to insure that his son was not the victim of the same kind of prejudice and exclusion that he had raged against decades earlier, Cleaver encountered a new struggle within himself.

He described a child he had noticed when he took his son to a regional day care center each afternoon after school. He saw that Riley, who typically had an embrace for everyone as he arrived at the center, always had a special kiss for one little girl. Cleaver admitted that he was repulsed by the little girl because she drooled constantly. Soon the little girl showed that she was happy to see both Riley and his father each day. At first there were just handshakes for Cleaver, then one day a hug and kiss were offered: "she stood up and came at me, and she was salivating, and I felt myself recoil. I looked at her face . . . and I realized that she was reaching out in faith. And I realized that it would be devastating to her if I . . . rejected her . . . that confrontation with myself was really a godsend, and it changed me again, and I embraced the little girl, and I'm so glad that I did that, because at that moment of resolving that, it gave me an insight into the condition of humanity!"[5]

THE ENRICHMENT OF DISABILITY

People with intellectual disabilities have the capacity to enrich our personal and social lives. The deficiency and defect models of disability have, however, clouded our ability to see their value. More than a decade ago Wolf Wolfensberger identified a number of strengths that people with intellectual disabilities may bring to their relationships with others. Among these attributes are:

- A natural and positive spontaneity.
- A tendency to respond to others generously and warmly.
- A tendency to respond honestly to others.
- The capacity to call forth gentleness, patience, and tolerance from others.
- A tendency to be trusting of others.[6]

Many of the disability "stories" I have told in my writing and in lectures, and many of those that have been told to me, include references to the positive characteristics of people with disabilities. When I reflect on the importance of these children and adults and their qualities, I find I must say something that I have often lacked the courage to say directly and publicly. To be disabled can be a valuable human attribute. People with disabilities can be powerful in the humanizing influence they have on others. I am glad I have had friends with disabilities for most of my life.

In his book *The Power of the Powerless,* Christopher de Vinck describes the experience of growing up with his brother, Oliver, who was born with multiple and severe disabilities. In his work as an English teacher de Vinck often told his students about his brother. "One day, during my first year of teaching, I was trying to describe Oliver's lack of response, how he had been spoon-fed every morsel he ever ate, how he never spoke. A boy in the last row raised his hand and said, 'Oh, Mr. de Vinck. You mean he was a vegetable' . . . Well, I guess you could call him a vegetable. I called him Oliver, my brother. You would have loved him."[7]

Christopher de Vinck describes Oliver as the weakest human being he ever met. The irony, however, is that he also describes his brother as one of the most powerful human beings he ever knew. When de Vinck assesses the effort and hope that go into teaching and writing and parenting, he thinks of the impact Oliver had on his life. "Oliver could do absolutely nothing except breathe, sleep, eat and yet he was responsible for action, love, courage and insight . . . [This] explains to a great degree why I am the type of husband, father, writer and teacher I have become."[8]

There is most certainly a human ecology of power and compassion. People with disabilities have an important place in that ecological balance. The power of those who have traditionally been considered powerless may be important to our health as human beings and as cultural groups. A person with a disability may temper hateful and prejudicial attitudes. A person with an intellectual disability may soften a heart that has become hardened. A person with multiple and severe disabilities may have much to teach us about love. John Lovelace had a profound impact on my life.

MY FRIEND JOHN

My friendship with John Lovelace is one that I valued greatly. This was true for several reasons. First, I liked him. He was a gentle and loving man who genuinely enjoyed being with others when he was able to communicate and share with them. I know that he was frustrated when he could not make himself understood, or when he had difficulty understanding the words and intentions of other people. A second reason John's friendship became important to me was that it kept me connected in a personal way to professional and academic pursuits in the human services that are my work. I was constantly challenged to think about what the things I studied and taught meant in the life of my friend.

I have told my students in recent years that my advice to them is to always have at least one person they are concerned about to whom they are not related in any way, and for whom they are not paid to be involved. I have come to believe we all need that kind of relationship to help keep alive our humanistic and altruistic impulses, and the motivation that originally brought many of us to the field of service to others. If we lose these values, we are at risk of our work becoming just another job. When this happens, we and those who depend on our advocacy and services suffer a great loss.

A third reason that John's friendship was such a special one for me was that it taught me so much about how reluctantly and slowly many of the human service systems in our society move. I have been involved with education and rehabilitation programs for children and adults with disabilities for more than 30 years. I have four academic degrees in fields that are all related to the education, counseling, and rehabilitation for people with special needs. Over the years I have established contacts with some of the most knowledgeable and influential people in the world in these fields. I have taught hundreds of undergraduate and graduate students. I have been a consultant to scores of projects. But when I faced the challenge of trying to help this one man in some very basic ways, I was largely unsuccessful or found the process to be painfully slow. My insider position made little difference in the life outcomes for John. As the preceding chapters illustrate, it took years to get minimal changes accomplished in his life.

In this regard my friendship with John gave me new insights about the painful experiences that many families of persons with disabilities encounter. I gained a deep appreciation for the constant struggle that these families may face. Even with this deepened appreciation, however, I still cannot imagine what the feelings of powerlessness and frustration must be for mothers, fathers, siblings, and friends who attempt to get the best help for those they love who have disabilities but have not had the benefit of the preparation that I have. I think that I also now understand those who are eventually worn down by the experience, those who give up, those who find themselves living with undeserved guilt, and those who abandon the hope that things can ever get better. I also think I understand those who become bitter and angry at the system, and at individual teachers, therapists, and other representatives of the service system. I think I came closer through John to sensing the special despair I had earlier seen in some families of children with disabilities, that sense of having been wronged by fate.

FLEETING FAME

I hoped the appearance of the article about John's life would somehow make an immediate difference. I suppose I had fantasies that the impact would be quick and profound. The *Roanoke Times and World-News* is read throughout the southwestern part of Virginia, and it is also one of the state's most important newspapers. I expected dramatic things would happen after the story appeared.

After more than six months at Draper Valley John was still not working at the sheltered workshop. No other program or service had been arranged. He seemed to be doing better in controlling his anger, but nothing else was happening. The administrator seemed like a concerned person, but it was not her role to arrange for any services outside the adult home. John was still inaccurately classified as being psychotic, and this continued to lead to confusion about who should be overseeing his case, what services he needed, or for which he was qualified. Repeated inquiries had brought no progress. Some of the professionals I spoke with seemed confused about who I was in relation to John and why I was calling or writing from more than a hundred miles away concerning him. Nothing was happening. I think I expected the newspaper article would be read by these same people, bringing recognition to John, and legitimacy to my interest in him.

The day before the article was published Frances Martin, the administrator at Draper Valley Rest Home, called my office. She said John wanted to talk with me. She put him on the line and we had a nice conversation. It was the first time I had received a call from him. Ms. Martin came back on the line and asked about the upcoming Camp Jaycee weekend and several other matters relating to John. I had the impression she had read the parts of Mike Hudson's series that had already appeared that week. I earlier told her to expect the article on John, and Mike had interviewed her. She probably was feeling some anxiety about what the article would say about Draper Valley Rest Home, but she didn't mention it. She said John had been doing very well and he just needed "someone to care about him." She also stressed that at Draper Valley "we love our residents." I mentioned the series, and she said then that she had been reading it and she thought it was "awful some of the things that go on." I asked her to watch for John's picture and story on Thursday. She said she would, and she would be certain that he saw it.

After the article was published I wrote to John. I had been pleased with the way Mike had written John's story and with the photographs. Several friends who knew about John and our relationship had commented on the power of the story and the potential impact it might have for John, and for bringing about some change in the adult home system in Virginia. People also commented on the importance of the whole series. Mike Hudson received many calls, and his stories were picked up by newspapers around the state. In my letter to John I tried to give him the credit he deserved for sharing his life story.

> I'm sure you saw your pictures in the *Roanoke Times and World-News.* I hope someone read the story to you. It was an important story and I think you should be proud. I think your life story being in the newspaper will help other people.
>
> I look forward to seeing you at Camp Virginia Jaycee on November 3rd. I will see what I can do about bringing a radio that you can take back to Draper Valley with you.
>
> I'm enclosing a few dollars which you may use as extra spending money. I hope it will help a little bit. I also hope that soon you will be able to work at the New River Valley Workshop. That will give you more money of your own. I know that is what you want.
>
> Tell Ms. Martin I said hello. I'm glad to hear that you are getting along so well with everyone. Take care and I will see you soon.
>
> Dave
>
> P.S. I will bring an extra copy of your picture and the article to Camp Jaycee for you to keep.

Mike Hudson's series on adult homes made a difference. The articles were read around the state, and interest was raised in initiating reform in the system. Mike did his job well. He is a fine journalist. I trusted that the interest that he stimulated among policy makers in Virginia would eventually help lead to the kinds of changes that were needed. Among the general public, however, the topic of adult homes captured a great deal of attention during the week that the series appeared, and then it quickly waned. For me this was an important lesson. We are so fickle in our culture with our attention to the media issues competing for our engagement. We view, read, and talk about issues as they pass through our filter of attention, and then we quickly move on to the next hot topic. I sometimes wonder about the true effect that the media bombardment we experience each day has on our sense of commitment to stay with problems and with people through to some point of action.

I did not expect there would be a flood of calls and letters to the newspaper asking how John Lovelace could be helped. Quite frankly, however, I did expect there would be a few. As far as I know, there were none. I thought there might be a note or two asking me for suggestions for helping John Lovelace, but there were none.

John was proud of the fact that he was in the newspaper. I was told later by Frances Martin that he was really impressed with the photographs. In another sense, however, John took his few minutes of fame in stride. In his dictated letter a few days later he said:

> I am doing real good at Draper. I help with mopping and sweeping. I get extra cigs and pop for helping. I like doing that.
>
> I have received your letter and money. That came in handy. I go to the store every day.
>
> Mrs. Martin (we call her Frances) said she was proud of me. That I was her big helper. She always hugs and tells me I am doing good. She kisses us [and] tells us that she cares for us alot. She gave me my pictures in the paper and the story. Sharon my friend is writing this letter for me. She writes for all of us. She lives upstairs.

RAYS OF LIGHT AND HOPE

There were to be other ways, however, that the article did serve John. By the first of December of 1989 John still had not even been evaluated for the possibility of working at the sheltered workshop. In fact, he had not been seen for the purpose of providing him with any sort of program or service. As far as I could determine, he was spending all of his time at Draper Valley dependent on the good graces of

Ms. Martin but with no meaningful contact with the outside community. I had become very frustrated, and I finally appealed to a friend within the state mental retardation system for help. He gave me the name of a person to write with the agreement that I would not discuss this with anyone else. To honor that request I will delete his name from the letter that I reprint here. It was his assistance, however, that led the way to some important improvements in John's life:

> ... I am writing to you at the suggestion of ... [He] speaks highly of you and felt you would be willing to try to help me with a concern that I have for a friend who is living at Draper Valley Rest Home. The enclosed article will give you background on John Lovelace and my relationship with him. I hope you can take the time to read it.
>
> For close to a year I have been attempting to help John with at least a trial placement at the New River Valley Workshop. I know that having employment there would mean a great deal to him in terms of the quality of his daily life, his self-esteem and having at least some income. So far I have been frustrated in this attempt. For some reason John has been placed under mental health rather than mental retardation. I really think that this is inappropriate since his primary diagnosis has always been mental retardation. Anyway, I have practically begged for information and assistance with little in the way of results. Sometimes my calls have not even been returned. I am not a person who is quick to complain and I believe that I have been patient and courteous with the person I have had contact with ... I don't want to cause difficulty for her. I just want to give John the best possible chance at an improved life.
>
> I would appreciate any assistance you might offer me. I know the holiday season is here and things are hectic. When you find time, however, would you please take a look at John's situation? Thanks in advance.

My letter was obviously written with a sense of frustration and exhaustion. I had grown weary of waiting for what I thought was to be forthcoming almost immediately when John moved. Even worse, I had seen no movement in the direction of his being allowed to work. I'm sure that similar letters have been written with a yield far less satisfying than I received. I was delighted when my concerns garnered a response from a former student of mine. Good luck and the interest generated by the copy of the article I sent with my letter began to intervene in John's life at this point in a way that would make a very real difference. The letter from my former student, Cathi Drinkard, made my day to say the least, and proved to be a turning point. She wrote:

> Dear Dr. Smith:
>
> My Director ... recently received your letter of December 12, 1989, and brought it to my immediate attention during a meeting yesterday. I am

most pleased to be able to assist you as you were of so much help to me during my graduate studies at Lynchburg College.

In regard to the matter that you addressed, allow me to explain what I have done so far. I have contacted Mr. Lovelace's Mental Health worker to ascertain why he is in their system instead of ours. It appears that when Mr. Lovelace came to Draper Valley Rest Home, no documentation accompanied him. Therefore, when his case was opened on July 5, 1988, he was given a mental health diagnosis of Intermittent Explosive Disorder based on the verbal information given regarding his history at other residences. The Mental Health worker stated that she had written Mr. Lovelace's previous residence, requesting additional information, but had not received anything to date.

After reading your letter and the attached article, it is obvious that Mr. Lovelace is mentally retarded. Therefore, in an attempt to obtain information that would make him eligible for services in our system, I have secured releases from Mr. Lovelace to request information from the Central Virginia Training Center, Burrell Home for Adults, Kennedy House, and Little Ponderosa Home for Adults. In addition, I have requested that Mr. Lovelace's Mental Health worker arrange for him to have a complete psychological done as soon as possible, which she has agreed to do.

Mr. Lovelace was referred to the Department of Rehabilitative Services to be screened for placement at the New River Valley Workshop several months ago by his Mental Health worker. [He] . . . has made contact with Mr. Lovelace and will be able to assist us more fully once information, such as a current psychological, has been obtained. I have asked one of my case managers to follow up on this to see if we can, perhaps, speed up this process.

I wanted to let you know where things stood at this point with Mr. Lovelace; as soon as further developments occur, I will contact you immediately. Mr. Lovelace is a lucky man to have a friend such as you; I know that he appreciates your concern and involvement, as do we as an agency . . .

One of the first valuable things that Cathi Drinkard did on John's behalf was to assign him to a case manager, who made all of the difference for him. Her name was Diane Williamson. Diane was more than a competent professional; she did her work with a sense of mission and personal commitment. During my first conversation with her I sensed that she would prove to be a real advocate for John. My initial impression proved to be accurate. More than any other one person, she did the important work that improved John's life.

By June of 1990 Diane had located a vacancy in what is the nicest adult home that I have ever visited. It was established as a nursing home decades ago by local philanthropists for the care of people with severe disabilities and the dependent elderly citizens of the small community of Dublin, Virginia. It was not very far from Draper Valley. John was cared for as well as resources would allow at Draper Valley, and I am convinced that he was cared about. But I was very happy when Diane was able to find a place for him at the Fairview Adult Home. It was clean and as cheerful as a place can be that is a home to people who are so different from the norm in health and life circumstances. The people who worked there seemed to genuinely care about the residents. And, as John told me in a letter shortly after he moved there, " . . . Fairview is nice to me. I usually go to the smoking room and then to my room. It's good food here, it's hot. They give me some more if I ask for it. I like it alright here."

CHAPTER 13

Ethics, Powerlessness, and Informed Consent

The classic fairy tales of Hans Christian Andersen and the Brothers Grimm are testaments to the enduring fascinations and fears that children have shared across the generations. The Grimm's *Hansel and Gretel* and *Cinderella*, and Andersen's *Ugly Duckling* and *The Emperor's New Clothes* continue to entertain children and to reassure them of the ultimate conquest of good over evil. There are other joys and anxieties of childhood, however, which are more generation specific. For the children of the new century, for example, terrorism, school violence, and the horror of AIDS has had an impact unimaginable to previous generations. The decade of the 1950s, on the contrary, is often portrayed as a period of idyllic childhood. What is forgotten in the nostalgic accounts of this period, however, is that along with Davy Crockett and coonskin caps, the children of the 1950s were taught to crouch under school desks in case of a Soviet nuclear attack. Another nightmare for the children of that generation was polio.

Polio, commonly called infantile paralysis because it most frequently affected children, reached epidemic proportions in the early 1950s. This viral disease paralyzed and killed thousands of children each year. Images of patients and the "iron lungs" used to enable them to breathe terrified both children and their parents. Although the means by which the disease was transmitted was uncertain, swimming pools were closed, public gatherings were avoided, and school cancellations were common during the worst outbreaks.

In early April 1955 newspaper headlines announced that a safe and effective polio vaccine had been developed by Dr. Jonas Salk. Before the end of that month, thousands of children were vaccinated against polio. By 1961, an oral vaccine for polio had been developed by Dr. Albert Sabin. In 1971, only one case of polio was documented in the United States.

POLIO MEMORIES

My personal reflections on the terrors of polio are embodied in three waves of thoughts and feelings. My first memory is of the death of a boy in my neighborhood. News that Billy had polio came as a shock to the community. He died within days. My parents' fears could not be concealed even from a six-year old. I accepted their restrictions willingly and played alone in my own backyard. I was terrified.

My second recollection is of standing in line for my first polio shot. I watched as some of my friends and classmates were inoculated, dreading my turn. That scene was to be repeated twice before the series of vaccinations was complete. The next time I was vaccinated was as an adult, this time with the Sabin technique. The sugar cube with a dot of vaccine was much more pleasant than the needle.

My final reflection on polio concerns the role of people with disabilities in the development of the polio vaccine. I became aware of their largely involuntary and exploitative participation in the research that led to the availability of the vaccine a few years ago. For my childhood peers and myself, the eradication of polio was a miracle. For people with disabilities and their advocates, the development of the vaccine is a disturbing saga. It is also a testament to the degree to which the lives of people with disabilities were devalued through most of the last century and into the current time. Reviewing the story may encourage us to think carefully as we look at the meaning of their lives in the future.

THE SALK VACCINE AND "INSTITUTIONALIZED" RESEARCH

Vaccination is accomplished by introducing a tiny amount of a virus into the body of the person being vaccinated. The immune system of that person responds by producing antibodies. The person vaccinated is thus protected against the "wild" form of the virus and the disease it causes. Vaccines may be created with either a weakened live virus or a dead virus. In general, both weakened and dead viruses produce antibodies but not the disease. Given the unique characteristics of a particular disease, however, either a live or a dead virus vaccine may not prove to be preventative. More importantly, some vaccines may actually produce the disease that is being targeted for immunity. Research and trials are important, therefore, in producing a safe yet effective vaccine.

Medical research is usually an evolutionary process. The work of one scientist provides a platform or stimulus for the research of the next. One of the pioneers in polio vaccine research was Howard Howe of Johns Hopkins University. In 1952, Dr. Howe produced a polio vaccine using a dead virus, which he tested on chimpanzees. It seemed to be safe and it produced antibodies against polio. Howe then tested the vaccine on children at the Rosewood Training School in Owings Mills, Maryland. He described these children as " . . . low grade idiots or imbeciles with congenital hydrocephalus, microcephaly, or cerebral palsy."[1] In reporting on the response to the vaccine, Howe wrote, "both children under five years of age and chimpanzees develop readily demonstrative neutralizing antibodies . . . following the injection of small quantities of . . . formalin inactivated poliomyelitis virus."[2]

Jonas Salk may have been inspired or nudged by Howe's work to move ahead more quickly with his own work on a vaccine for polio. He might also have been influenced by Howe's research in his selection of subjects for trial vaccinations. Salk had tried his vaccine on animals, and it appeared to be safe and effective. In a 1952 article, he described testing his vaccine at the D. T. Watson Home for Crippled Children in Pennsylvania. Some of the children he vaccinated had already been disabled by polio and, therefore, had some level of immunity. Others had no immunity at all to the disease. In both groups, Salk found that his vaccine promoted the development of antibodies.[3]

Salk continued his research at the Polk State School in Pennsylvania, where he vaccinated institutionalized children. The antibody production stimulated by the vaccine in this group was also encouraging. He was relieved by the fact that none of the children contracted polio, a risk associated with the vaccine since some undetectable amount of virus might not have been killed. Salk was quoted as saying, "When you inoculate children with polio vaccine, you don't sleep well for two or three months."[4]

FEEDING LIVE POLIO VIRUS TO CHILDREN WITH DISABILITIES

The fact that children and adults with disabilities were the subjects of choice for medical research at the time of Salk's work on polio is made even more clear through the trials that led to the development of a live virus vaccine. Although the name of Albert Sabin is most often associated with this vaccine, a number of scientists were involved in its development. In fact, a competition developed between researchers for the discovery of the most reliable and effective live virus oral vaccine. Sabin won the competition, but the race could have been won by Hilary Koprowski.

The quest for a reliable live virus vaccine was stimulated by two factors. One, a live virus vaccine could be administered orally rather than being injected. This would make it less expensive and easier to immunize large numbers of people. Second, Salk's dead virus vaccine had not proven to be as effective as originally thought. There were cases where the dead virus did not create immunity. There were also cases where the techniques for killing the virus had not been totally effective. Live virus that remained in the vaccine in these instances caused polio in some of the people injected with it.

Like Salk and Sabin, Hilary Koprowski set out on a very personal mission to eradicate polio. Even before the successful development of Salk's vaccine, Koprowski was testing weakened but still living strains of polio virus. He tested the vaccine on monkeys, but he also revealed in a 1951 meeting that he had administered a live polio virus vaccine to human subjects.

In his report of feeding the virus to 20 children with intellectual disabilities at Letchworth Village in New York, Koprowski explained that his decision to administer the virus to humans for the first time was based on "gaps in knowledge concerning the mechanisms of infection and immunity in poliomyelitis ... due to the fact that, as far as is known, human beings have never been exposed to actual administrations of living poliomyelitis virus for clinical trial purposes."[5] Arthur Klein reported in his description of the trial of the vaccine that Koprowski requested permission of the New York State Department of Health to test it on the children at Letchworth. In fact, Koprowski did not request permission. In his later account of the trials, Koprowski provided the following recollections:

> I realized then that I would never get official permission from the State of New York. Therefore, we asked permission from the parents of those children. The parents gave us permission to feed vaccine to their children. On February 17, 1950 the first human subject was immunized with poliomyelitis virus by drinking an emulsion ...[6]

Koprowski described the vaccinated children at Letchworth Village as "volunteers." In fact, "Volunteer No. 1" was a six-year-old boy with severe disabilities who had to be fed the vaccine through a stomach tube. The other 19 "volunteers" had similar multiple disabilities. There was no mention in the original report of parental permission having been sought or granted.

Fortunately none of the children at Letchworth developed polio from swallowing the live virus vaccine. Koprowski reported that they all developed antibodies. It is clear, however, that he gambled with the lives of those children. The vaccine strain had been problematic in tests with monkeys. In those earlier trials, in fact, half of the subjects were paralyzed and a quarter of them died.

In discussing his memories of the meeting where he first disclosed his Letchworth Village research, Koprowski referred to Albert Sabin's reaction:

> Sabin was quite vociferous at the meeting . . . he questioned my daring. How did I dare to feed children live polio virus? I replied that somebody had to take this step. Well, he turned round and round saying, "How do you dare to use live virus on children? You are not sure about this, you are not sure about that, you may have caused an epidemic."[7]

Koprowski was also criticized in the medical journal *Lancet* for the lack of evidence that he had obtained truly informed consent for his subjects.

> Koprowski et. al. tells us in a footnote that for obvious reasons the age, sex, and physical status of each volunteer are not mentioned. The reasons must be more obvious to the authors than to the reader, who can only guess, from the methods used for feeding the virus, that the volunteers were very young and that the volunteering was done by their parents. One of the reasons for the richness of the English language is that the meaning of some words is continually changing. Such a word is "volunteer." We may yet read in a scientific journal that an experiment was carried out with twenty volunteer mice, and that 20 other mice volunteered as controls.[8]

This criticism and sarcasm, however, does not seem to have deterred Koprowski. Subsequent investigations of the records from a conference on the "Biology of Poliomyelitis" indicate that several further trials of live virus vaccine were very likely conducted at Letchworth, although they were not published in the mainstream medical literature.

KOPROWSKI AND THE CHILDREN OF SONOMA

It is certain, however, that Koprowski conducted his vaccine research on children with intellectual disabilities elsewhere. In July

1952, Koprowski tested his oral vaccine on 61 children at Sonoma State Hospital in California, all of them having mental retardation as their primary diagnosis. The children ranged in age from eight months to eight years of age. This time Koprowski made certain that he had formal permission to conduct his research. With the help of physicians at Sonoma, the appropriate clearance was swiftly obtained from California authorities. The trial was considered a success when 52 of the 61 children showed an increase in antibody levels to polio.

In the course of the vaccine research, Koprowski and his colleagues conducted another study. This experiment is particularly revealing of the attitudes toward children with disabilities that were prevalent during the research. Koprowski reported that a group of six children who had been fed the vaccine were, as a result, excreting virus in their stools. He described them as being kept "in very intimate contact" with another eight children who lacked antibodies. In fact, the children (who were incontinent) were allowed to play together three hours a day on a plastic mat which, although washed down to remove gross soils, was deliberately not disinfected. In the course of this experiment, three of the unvaccinated children became infected with the virus. None of the nurses, however, developed antibodies. Koprowski reasoned that the nurses caring for the children took precautions against infection, wearing protective clothing and washing their hands after every contact with a child. Koprowski also concluded that the vaccine virus was not contagious "when the principles of simple personal hygiene are practiced ... " Again, the disregard for the children as human beings is evident in his report.[9]

Koprowski continued his research on institutionalized populations, including other children with mental retardation and the infants of female prison inmates, for several years. In 1957 and 1958, he enlarged his research to include thousands of children in Africa and Russia. His vaccine fell into disfavor, however, when polio cases in Northern Ireland were linked to his research there. Ultimately Albert Sabin would win the oral vaccine race, and his form of live virus was adopted for use in the United States.

RESEARCH AND DISABILITIES: OTHER CASES

As disturbing as the history of the polio vaccine trials are, there are other examples of children and adults with disabilities being used as devalued subjects in medical research. As described in an earlier chapter, during the 1940s and through the 1950s, children and adults at Fernald State School were used in a scientific study conducted by the

Massachusetts Institute of Technology on the nutritional effects of ingesting radioactive iron.[10,11] Children who received permission from their parents to join the "Science Club" were fed oatmeal laced with the radiated metal. From 1946 to 1952, over 125 children were exposed to radiation at the Fernald School in this manner.

The Willowbrook State School was another setting in which the questionable use of persons with disabilities in medical research occurred. The Willowbrook studies were conducted from the 1950s to the 1970s, and they sought to identify a vaccine for hepatitis. A research team systematically infected residents with varying strands of hepatitis, knowing that those children would develop the infectious disease.

The value placed on people with disabilities by some researchers is evident in their choice of human subjects rather than animals. According to the Humane Society, institutionalized children were used for research purposes because they were "cheaper than calves."[12] During the polio trials, the cost of raising and keeping monkeys for experimental use was so high that doctors frequently sought human "volunteers." Children were given an experimental vaccine after it had been tested on only 62 animals.

In the cases of the Fernald radiation studies and the Willowbrook hepatitis experiment, the validity of the parental consent obtained is questionable. According to the permission letter to the parents in the Fernald experiment, the benefits of the Science Club consisted of receiving an extra quart of milk each day, attendance at baseball games, and trips to the beach. There was no mention in the parental consent letter of the radiation experiments nor of the potential harm that could come to their children.

Consent in the Willowbrook studies was also obtained in a questionable manner. Parents were asked for consent and were promised that their children would be placed on a special ward with extra staff. The researchers failed to tell the parents that the special ward was for individuals infected with hepatitis.

CLAIMING A PLACE OF VALUE: THE CONTINUING STRUGGLE

Jonas Salk won a victory over the polio epidemic. Albert Sabin won the race for an oral vaccine. Millions of people in the world benefited from these triumphs. It is critical, however, that we reflect on the struggle that continues for people with disabilities in claiming their human worth in the eyes of their fellow human beings. Perhaps the sacrifices that these people have made for others will eventually be recognized and their value in society secured. Until then, their friends, families, and advocates cannot rest.

In 1981 a pair of conjoined twins, children most often referred to as Siamese twins, were born to a woman in Danville, Illinois. The father of the twins was a physician. The infants, who were joined below the waist, were not given the immediate medical treatment they needed to optimize their chances of survival. Nourishment was also withheld from them. Withholding medical care and nourishment was done by the hospital on the order of the parents. They felt that it was best that the twins be allowed to die because of their condition. The State of Illinois interceded in the case and was awarded custody of the children. The parents and their pediatrician were indicted for attempted murder. They were not, however, convicted of the charge.[13]

In 1982 an infant with Down syndrome was born in Bloomington, Indiana. The child had an additional complication. His esophagus was not completely developed. Nourishment could not pass through this malformed tube into the baby's stomach. The condition was completely correctable through surgery. The parents of the child, however, refused to grant permission for the operation to be performed. They felt that death was preferable to the survival of the child because of his intellectual disability. Their decision was upheld by several courts. The child, who had become known as Baby Doe, died before a final judicial appeal could be completed.[14]

A baby girl who came to be called Baby Jane Doe was denied surgery in 1983. This child was born with the multiple disabilities of spina bifida and hydrocephalus. There were also other physical complications, and she was diagnosed as mentally retarded. A Long Island judge ruled that life-prolonging surgery should be performed on the child even though this was not the wish of the parents. An appeals court supported the will of the parents and overturned the lower court decision.[15]

During the last two decades the number of cases like these that came to the attention of the public increased to the point that withholding of treatment and nourishment from newborns with severe disabilities became a political issue. During the Reagan administration orders were issued to hospitals and medical personnel restricting the practice of pediatric euthanasia and providing mechanisms for reporting suspected or known cases. Although public attention was drawn to this issue during the 1980s, it was not a practice that had its origins during that time. In 1973 researchers R. S. Duff and A. G. Campbell reported in *The New England Journal of Medicine* that 14 percent of the infants that died in the Yale-New Haven Medical Center from January 1970 to January 1972 died as a result of the intentional withholding of treatment.[16] A similar article published in the *Archives of Childhood Disease* in 1982 reported comparable results from a study in a British hospital. That article, entitled "Which Infants Should Not Receive Intensive Care?" showed that over 20 percent of the infant deaths in that hospital resulted from decisions to withdraw or withhold treatment. According to the article, "Simply stated, about one-fifth of all neonatal deaths or 1-2 infants for every 1,000 infants born alive are being allowed to die."[17] Even these figures may not adequately portray the actual magnitude of the question of pediatric euthanasia. One study found that of infant deaths in an intensive care nursery physicians cited quality of life concerns for limiting treatment in 51% of the cases.[18] Although a significant number of these children would certainly have died even with the best of treatment and the most heroic measures, many observers believe that the practice of withholding treatment and life sustaining nourishment is causing the deaths of an increasing number of infants each year.

A QUESTION OF HUMANHOOD

In discussions of the ethics of medical care for newborns with severe disabilities or who are otherwise seriously ill, a common theme concerns the projected quality of life of these infants. Advocates of the quality-of-life position argue that decisions concerning euthanasia should be based on the prospective enjoyment and meaningfulness that the person in question is likely to derive by continuing to live. This, they argue, must be weighed against the suffering the person is expected to experience and the degree to which he or she will be a burden to the family and to society. From this perspective human life is defined essentially by factors of "fitness" to live.

The philosopher and ethicist Joseph Fletcher was a strong proponent of the quality of life position. In his book entitled *Humanhood: Essays in Biomedical Ethics,* for example, he listed criteria which should be met before a life would be considered to be of human quality. His list included the following criteria:

- Minimal intelligence (an IQ higher than 20)
- Self awareness
- Self control
- A sense of time
- A sense of the past

- The capacity to relate to others
- Concern for others
- Communication
- Control of existence
- Curiosity
- A balance of rationality[19]

As I described earlier, I have worked in special education and rehabilitation settings for many years. If these criteria were strictly applied to children and adults with disabilities that I have seen develop into happy and productive people, most of them would not be considered human. The social, intellectual, and physical challenges which they have faced would interfere with their performance in most of the areas listed by Fletcher. Taking this perspective on their disabilities would result in their being viewed as not meeting the criteria for humanhood. Indeed, Fletcher contended, for example, that any individual with Down syndrome is not a person. He argued that an individual with the social and intellectual limitations associated with "mongolism" (an unfortunate and racist term applied to those people) is simply not, according to his criteria, a human personality.

If all of these qualities and abilities must be manifested in an individual or must be reasonably expected to be manifested by the time the person reaches maturity in order to pass the quality of life test, many seemingly well-functioning adults would surely fail to qualify as human beings. In fact, I am convinced that there would be numbers of individuals with advanced degrees that I have known who would fail this test!

A major concern with the quality-of-life position on pediatric euthanasia centers on the elasticity of the term "quality." Some critics fear that it can be arbitrarily invoked against people who have no power to defend themselves. That there are individuals against whom judgments of life quality are otherwise made on a daily basis is undeniable. A culture that overly values youth will devalue people who are considered old. A culture that sets narrow standards of beauty will devalue people that it considers to be ugly. A culture that worships wealth will devalue those who are poor. A culture that narrowly defines productivity will look down on those who are considered unproductive. A culture that is obsessed with personal independence will devalue those who are dependent, in some cases even its very young and very old. Professor Wolf Wolfensberger of Syracuse University has argued that all devalued people are literally in danger of their lives. He feels that people whose social roles have not been "valorized," assigned some value rather than being devalued, are constantly at risk.[20]

In the case of infants who are born with disabilities there is the danger that arbitrary standards for life quality will influence decisions made about their care and treatment. There is also the likelihood that prejudice and bias will influence predictions of which infants would be likely to eventually meet those standards in their later development. Physicians and parents alike may be more influenced by misconceptions and stereotypes about disabilities than by factual information about the realities of the lives of people with disabilities. Prognostications concerning the quality of life of a newborn with disabilities may be overly pessimistic.

Those most often involved in the decision of whether an infant with a disability should be denied treatment or nourishment are parents, physicians, and, in cases that become public, the courts. Arguments have been made both for and against the roles of each of these parties in making such decisions.

WHO DECIDES?

Support for parents as decision makers usually derives from the concept that the well-being of children is primarily a matter for the judgment of parents, and that they have the final voice in any crucial matter concerning their progeny. Critics of this view believe that parents are often emotionally distraught and lack adequate information on which to base their decision when faced with such a dilemma. Their decisions may be largely influenced by their fears concerning raising the child, concerns about the impact of the disabled child on other family members, and anxiety over the continuing dependencies of the child into adult life.

Physicians are often perceived to be in the most informed and appropriate position for making an objective decision concerning pediatric euthanasia. It has been observed, however, that they may in fact be most often motivated by their opinions of what will prevent suffering in the family. They may, therefore, be acting more as the agent for the family than as the physician for the infant. With this conflict of roles in mind, it has been argued that physicians should not be the decision makers in these situations as it is their duty to preserve life rather than make judgments about which lives deserve preservation.

Courts become involved in life-and-death decisions about newborns with disabilities through the question of whether or not a child with a disability is entitled to the same protection under the law as any other citizen. The behavior of courts in such cases has been less than consistent. In some cases they have ordered extraordinary forms of treatment. In other instances they have allowed non-treatment of easily correctable physical problems which resulted in the death of an infant.[21]

As discussed earlier, the beginning of public awareness of the issue of pediatric euthanasia and newborns with disabilities goes back to the early 1970s. The case that became most visible and which stirred considerable controversy was that of a child born with Down syndrome at Johns Hopkins University Hospital. The infant began vomiting shortly after he was born. Further examination disclosed the existence of a blockage in the child's intestinal tract, a condition referred to as duodenal atresia. This blockage could have been removed surgically with minimal risk to the baby. Not removing it meant that normal digestion and nourishment of the child's body was impossible. The decision in the Johns Hopkins case was to withhold treatment. The parents of the child decided not to have the surgery performed. The child was otherwise in normal health except for the atresia and showing the physical characteristics of Down syndrome. Following the parent's decision, all feeding and fluid tubes were disconnected from the child. He died 15 days later of starvation and dehydration.[22]

Surely this is a case of life-and-death discrimination against a child because of an intellectual disability. He died because, in addition to the duodenal atresia, he was a child who was by definition disabled. A child with duodenal atresia who did not show evidence of Down syndrome would without question have been given the appropriate surgery, even if it were against the wishes of the parents.

WHICH VOICES SHOULD BE HEARD?

In 2002 the American Association on Mental Retardation (now the American Association on Intellectual and Developmental Disabilities) responded to this and similar cases with the following position statement:

> Disability must not be a factor in the decision to provide, delay, or withhold treatments or to provide or receive organ transplants. The person's medical condition and welfare must be the basis for the decision.[23]

The American Association on Intellectual and Developmental Disabilities (AAIDD) is a professional organization composed of members from many different professions. It has been strongly affiliated with and supported by a membership of educators, psychologists, physicians, administrators, and others who are involved with research and service in the field of intellectual disabilities. The 2002 position statement was an updating of its resolution in 1983 that asserted:

> It is the position of the ... Association ... that the existence of mental retardation is no justification for terminating the life of a human being or for permitting such a life to be terminated either directly or through the withholding of life-sustaining procedures.[24]

However, the organization whose membership has been primarily composed of special educators focused on the education and training of persons with intellectual disabilities is the Developmental Disabilities Division of the Council for Exceptional Children. I have been a member of both organizations for many years. The issue of pediatric euthanasia is an important one for professionals in the field of special education. The Johns Hopkins case and others have been cited widely in college and graduate school classrooms for over three decades as illustrations of ethical dilemmas of concern to special educators.

In most undergraduate and graduate training programs students preparing to become special educators are presented with the idea that part of their professional role will be that of an advocate, a voice, for the rights of people with disabilities. When faced with the question of pediatric euthanasia of infants with disabilities, however, the question of the nature and extent of the role of the special educator as advocate has been viewed as more complex and difficult by professionals in the field. Expressing a position on a matter that has traditionally been viewed as the province of parents, physicians, and the courts has been awkward and troubling to many people in the field.

Through conversations with my colleagues, however, I became convinced that the voice of teachers needed to be somehow heard on this issue. Parents, physicians, lawyers, and judges have rarely had the experience of living or working with individuals with intellectual disabilities to the extent that special educators do. Teachers serving people with disabilities from infancy through adulthood have the opportunity to observe that an intellectual disability, in the absence of severe and chronic disease, or other physical problems, does not necessarily cause a life of pain, suffering, or absence of a quality life.

These professionals are also able to see, through direct experience with persons who have intellectual disabilities, that this should not imply justification, in and of itself, for the termination of life.

Interaction with people having these disabilities tends to convince their families, teachers, and others who come to know them well that all people can learn, all can participate to some degree in the wide range of human experiences, and that most can become valuable citizens of whatever niche in society that they come to inhabit. In other words, they become truly valued by people who have the opportunity to genuinely know them.

With these thoughts in mind, and after more conversations with one of my closest colleagues, Dr. Ed Polloway, I asked the board of directors of what was then known as the Mental Retardation Division of the Council for Exceptional Children to consider approving a position statement on the rights of people with mental retardation to medical care and treatment to sustain their lives. The following position statement was approved by the Board in June of 1988 and published in the journal *Education and Training of the Mentally Retarded* in March of 1989:

> The Board of Directors of the Division on Mental Retardation of the Council for Exceptional Children resolves that the fact that a person is born with mental retardation or acquires mental retardation during development is not a justifiable reason, in and of itself, for terminating the life of that person. Mental retardation alone is not a nullification of quality or worth in an individual's life and should not be used as a rationale for the termination of life through direct means nor the withholding of nourishment or life-sustaining procedures.[25]

The board of directors of the Mental Retardation Division of the Council for Exceptional Children asked that I write an article to accompany the position statement. I did so, and it was published with the statement under the title "On the Right of Children with Mental Retardation to Life Sustaining Medical Care and Treatment: A Position Statement."[26] Even though I was already deeply involved with John Lovelace's life experiences at that time, it did not occur to me to mention in the article that this was an issue that touched on the lives of both children and adults with intellectual disabilities. If I could rewrite the article I would include that critical observation.

The issue of making life-and-death decisions about adults with intellectual disabilities is essentially the same as those for children. Again, it may be the parents (or other family members), physicians, and courts that become involved, and the concerns expressed earlier about each of these parties to the process may apply. In other cases, however, an adult with an intellectual disability may not have family members who can be found to participate in the decision making. This may be particularly true for the older residents of institutions and those in community placements.

In some cases the decision to give or withhold treatment may rest with a group of professionals charged with examining individual situations and making recommendations to an institutional administrator or legal counsel. It seems ironic to me that I found that the rights of the remaining residents of some large state institutions were more carefully protected in this regard than the people who were discharged into community placements. In part, de-institutionalization was motivated by concerns over the risks of impersonalization and abuse in institutional settings. Yet those who remained in them may have been safer from these dangers than those who were removed to the community! I believe that this was the reality in John Lovelace's case.

INFORMED CONSENT

A pivotal concept that has come to be employed in treatment decisions is "informed consent." In the case of children with intellectual disabilities, it is accepted that the parents have the right to informed consent and the right to understand adequately the likely consequences of treatment (or non-treatment) options for their child, and for the rest of their family. Obviously, in these cases the quality and completeness of the information that is made available to them is critical. This raises questions about who is competent to provide information concerning a child's projected future and what safeguards are needed in the procedure of providing information.

Again, the same considerations are important for adults with intellectual disabilities. In John's case, did the physician explain in detail the meaning of the no-code order that he presented to John? Even if he did go through the motions of explanation, did John understand what he was being told? Even if he understood the information, was he intimidated in his decision by having the authority figure of a physician suggest to him that this was the proper thing to do?

Informed consent is such an important and complex process in the provision of information to people with intellectual disabilities and to their families in making treatment decisions that the American Association on Mental Retardation published a *Consent Handbook* in 1977. The *Consent Handbook* defined informed consent as having three elements: capacity, information, and voluntariness. From this perspective informed consent must have all three of these elements in order for it to be considered valid.

The first element, capacity, is determined by considering three factors: the age of the person, the competence of the person, and the particular situation. Obviously, the age of a child makes it necessary that the parents or guardians be involved in the granting of informed consent. An infant cannot be active in the process at all, and an older child might be involved with the parents in the decision to some extent. A person who has reached legal majority (usually 18 years old), but who has intellectual disabilities, may still come under the guardianship of her or his parents. Informed consent may still need to come through the parents in this case. This is due to the second factor of competence. If the person has been judged to be incompetent to give informed consent, then age becomes an insufficient measure of capacity. The third factor, the particular situation, may become relevant to the question of capacity when considering the circumstance of the person with retardation who has no next of kin or guardian, and where a professional or committee must participate in a more independent way in determining what is in the best interest of this individual.[27]

John Lovelace signed a document, a no-code order, that indicated that he did not wish to receive treatment to save his life in a medical emergency. It documented that in the case of a stroke or heart attack it was his wish that his life not be saved. Although he had been diagnosed as mentally retarded and had lived in an institution for more than 20 years, he had never been declared incompetent and he did not have a legal guardian. He had no trace of a family. John Lovelace had the legal right to sign the document, but I do not believe that he had the capacity to make the decision that it reflected. I think that asking him to sign it was a social travesty. I fear that many other people in the same circumstances have been asked, and are being asked, to do the same. I believe that it is wrong.

The second part of consent as defined by the *Consent Handbook* is information. This concerns both what information is given and how it is given.[28] It is important that the person be told fully and accurately the consequences of treatment options. It is also important that the person be given this information in a manner that is comprehensible given their background and capacity. I do not know, of course, what transpired during the conversation between the physician and John concerning the no-code order, but I do know how difficult it has been at times for me to explain to him things far less complex than a life-or-death decision. It seems to me that this would be an ultimate challenge in communication. I hope that it is perceived to be so by anyone who would accept that challenge.

On page 10 of the *Consent Handbook* the author, Rud Turnbull, speaks about the third part of informed consent, voluntariness. He says that in order for the person to be voluntarily consenting he or she must be able to exercise free choice without force, deceit, or coercion.[29] With few exceptions, John's life was filled with events of force and coercion. He surely encountered deceit as well. He learned that his only means of assertion and defense was lashing out in very elemental, and ultimately self destructive ways. He felt very little free power of choice. He lived most of his life in settings where almost everyone had more power than he did. John lived a life of routines prescribed for him by professionals and others who made decisions about what seemed best for him. I am certain that he would have signed any document that I asked him to sign. I suspect that he did the same for the physician. I am certain that thousands of powerless people in similar circumstances have done the same.

By the time of her death in 2005 Terry Schiavo had become the focus of attention of the press, of politicians, and of the Vatican. When courts ruled that her husband could have her feeding tube removed, President George W. Bush expressed outrage. Ms. Schiavo had been in a coma for more than 15 years. Her husband decided that the most loving act would be to release her from what physicians referred to as a persistent vegetative state.[30] When I read accounts of the controversy and Michael Schiavo's decision I reflected on the circumstances of my meeting John Lovelace years ago and the circumstances of my saying goodbye to him more recently. I will have more to say about that farewell later.

CHAPTER 14

Blindness and Finding Yourself in Purgatory

In his book *Inventing the Feeble Mind,* James Trent described mental retardation as a:

> construction whose changing meaning is shaped both by individuals who initiate and administer policies, programs and practices, and by the social context to which these individuals are responding.[1]

As discussed earlier, Trent argued that the meaning of *disabilities* has sometimes been constructed in the name of science, sometimes in the name of caring for people with disabilities, and sometimes in the name of social or economic necessity. Each of these reasons for describing people with disabilities, however, has also been used for the purpose of controlling people who are perceived to be a threat or an inconvenience to society. The construction of the meaning of *disability* has, from this perspective, been motivated more by a search for control than by a concern for the best interests of people with disabilities.

HELEN KELLER: A MAGNIFICENT EXCEPTION

There have been, of course, exceptions to prevalent social constructions of the meaning of *disabilities.* These exceptions have most often occurred when an individual with a disability achieved prominence, and visibility, through extraordinary accomplishments. Helen Keller is an outstanding example of a person with severe disabilities but through magnificent achievements was able to eclipse the prevailing attitudes about people with those disabilities. Her life and her relationship with her teacher Annie Sullivan are inspiring and worthy of study. In his biography of Helen, Joseph Lash observed that her disabilities may have been necessary vehicles for the achievement of her extraordinary insight and influence. He quoted one of her contemporaries as having speculated on what she might have accomplished if she had not been blind and deaf, and then added that perhaps these were the differences that created her "high intelligence and purity of soul." Helen agreed, saying, "I have made my limitations tools of learning and true joy."[2]

Some years ago I made a discovery while working on a research project in the Manuscript Division of the Library of Congress. I happened upon a reference to letters from and to Helen Keller in the Alexander Graham Bell Collection. As I looked through these papers, I became enthralled with them. Here were letters actually written by Helen, Annie Sullivan, Alexander Graham Bell, and others that presented a unique and important view of Helen, her friendships, and her philosophy.

I soon shared these letters with the wonderful colleague who served as a mentor to so many of my generation, Burton Blatt. Burt read the letters, just as he approached most things, with vigor, insight, and depth of feeling. We discussed his using the letters in a manuscript, and I encouraged him to do so. He subsequently cited some of the letters in an article that was published shortly after his death.

In that article Blatt quoted extensively from several of the letters. He prefaced these excerpts by explaining that he chose them primarily to draw lessons from these glimpses into the relationship between Helen and Annie Sullivan, her beloved teacher. One quotation that he did not include in his article but that I think portrays the dedication of "Teacher," as Helen always called her, and the epiphany that she created in her student's life was contained in a letter of July 5, 1918. Helen wrote to Alexander Graham Bell describing the moment when she understood that the finger-spelling that she felt in her hand had meaning.

> Sometimes I feel that in that supreme moment she thought me into being … My fingers still glow with the feel of the first word that opened its golden heart to me. How everything seemed to think, to live! Shall I, in all the years of eternity, forget the torrent of wonders that rushed upon me out of the darkness and silence?[3]

HELEN KELLER AND THE PARAMETERS OF ADVOCACY

In his article, Blatt referred to the breadth of Helen Keller's advocacy for the rights of many of the world's most troubled people. She became a political activist and spokesperson for the victims of poverty, economic exploitation, gender bias, and other forms of oppression. Burt described Helen's advocacy as follows:

> As she strove to free herself from the difficulties which disease created in her, she more and more sought to understand the difficulties which society created for mankind's downtrodden multitudes.[4]

Blatt had a keen sense of history. He understood that the facts and personalities of any historical period are intimately entwined with the social and philosophical context of that period. He also understood that a seemingly clear "good guy-bad guy" dichotomy in the study of any historical topic is likely to be incorrect. He understood that "real" history is fraught with contradictions and disappointments. He knew that this was particularly true of the study of the history of mental retardation.[5]

My own sense of the contradictory nature of the study of history of intellectual disabilities was challenged recently as I was reading a fascinating book entitled *The Black Stork*. The author, Martin Pernick, provided an interesting account of a controversy that began in 1915 and that surrounded the work of a physician who openly practiced euthanasia on "defective" newborns. Dr. Harry Haiselden not only allowed infants with severe disabilities to die, he also administered drugs to speed the death of several of these newborns. He also campaigned for the widespread adoption of these practices and produced and starred in a movie promoting euthanasia, "The Black Stork." The film was based on Haiselden's eugenic arguments and was shown in commercial movie theaters from 1916 through the 1920s.[6]

In reading about this controversy, I was intrigued by a reference made to Helen Keller's support of Haiselden's eugenic campaign. When I reviewed her position on the euthanasia of infants with intellectual disabilities, my perception of the contradictory nature of historical realities, and my sense of Helen Keller as a person of her time, was deepened.

In her statement Keller expressed the following opinions:

> It is the possibilities of happiness, intelligence and power that give life its sanctity, and they are absent in the case of a poor, misshapen, paralyzed, unthinking creature ... The toleration of such anomalies tends to lessen the sacredness in which normal life is held.

It seems to me that the simplest, wisest thing to do would be to submit cases like that of the malformed idiot baby to a jury of expert physicians ... A mental defective ... is almost sure to be a potential criminal. The evidence before a jury of physicians considering the case of an idiot would be exact and scientific. Their findings would be free from the prejudice and inaccuracy of untrained observation. They would act only in case of true idiocy, where there could be no hope of mental development.[7]

CONTRADICTIONS AND "GOOD" HISTORY

Considering the history of mental retardation, Blatt wrote that:

virtually all histories in our field are dangerously incomplete ... That which is preserved may be less relevant than that which is unknown; and the 'facts,' however pertinent, are to a degree divorced from the social-psychological context of the period ... To understand what actually occurred (and why) requires one to know what the times were like.[8]

Helen Keller's development as an intellectual and as an advocate took place within the context of the scientific/social movement of eugenics. It also occurred within the political/philosophical environment of progressivism. Progressive thought held that most of the problems of society and those of individuals could and should be reduced to scientific terms, and resolved by scientific means. Helen's trust of a "jury" of physicians is very consistent with the faith in scientific progress that characterized the cultural climate of her formative years as a social activist. Her opinion that "true idiocy" lessens the sanctity of "normal life" reflects the eugenic principles to which she was certainly exposed. These arguments supported euthanasia, sterilization, and institutionalization. They asserted that these and other eugenic measures were in the best interests of both society and the "defective" individual.

Helen's voice of advocacy was bold for its time. It was focused, however, on the potential for social intercourse and productivity in the lives of ignored, misunderstood, and exploited people. In that regard, she moved beyond a social context that devalued many people with blindness, deafness, and other physical disabilities, for example, and crusaded for their rights to earn a place in society. She was a courageous advocate for these people and she deserves the admiration embodied in Blatt's tribute to her:

Seeing with her hands and her soul while others could see only with their eyes, she was led to the idea of a new social order, a world free of worker exploitation, free of preventable disease, free of sexism, free of all forms of human oppression.[9]

BURTON BLATT'S ADVOCACY: THE GOLDEN RULE AND BEYOND

Burt Blatt's advocacy, like that of Helen Keller, was grounded in a commitment to human rights and human dignity. In his voice, however, rights were not couched in the expectation of productivity and dignity was not contingent on independence. He urged that advocates work for others not as they would have others treat them but as they would treat themselves in the most challenging of circumstances.

Ironically, Burt's voice as an advocate is heard clearly in his description of the relationship between Helen Keller and Annie Sullivan. He believed that before Helen was liberated to become a brilliant and famous person, she was a person with mental retardation. He felt that the fact that she functioned like a person with an intellectual disability was one of the two most central facets of the "miracle' of her life story. The second central facet of the story, according to Burt, was that Annie's commitment as Helen's teacher was unconditional. When Sullivan boarded a train in Boston destined for Tuscumbia, Alabama, it was not with the expectation that Helen would become a miracle student and she a miracle worker. In describing Annie's commitment and advocacy, Blatt said:

> Indeed, had Annie spent her entire life with Helen, and had Helen never made a single intelligible response, everything we know about Annie Sullivan suggests that she would not have felt that her life was wasted.[10]

LEGACIES AND CHALLENGES

Through the memory of Helen Keller and Annie Sullivan, we are challenged to hold firm to a belief in the miracle of commitments that are unconditional and sustained. We are also reminded of the contradictions that characterize history and even the greatest of personalities. Through Burt Blatt's mentorship, we are strengthened by a legacy of hopefulness. We are challenged to believe that the conquest of disabilities is possible.

A HOPEFUL FRIEND

Diane Williamson truly became a friend to John Lovelace, in addition to being a very competent case manager with the New River

Valley Community Services Board. It was through her efforts that he eventually went to work at the New River Valley Workshop. Finally he was able to do what he had been practically begging for, he was going to be working! His involvement at the Workshop was initially an extended period of evaluation to determine his level of abilities and the kind of work that he would be best suited for there. He seemed to enjoy this and apparently worked hard at doing well at the various tasks he was given. After only a short while, however, there was an interruption in his involvement with the Workshop. He broke his glasses again and was unable to see well enough to function in work activities. It took several weeks to get his glasses repaired, and by then John was anxious to get back to work. In a letter I received from him in July of 1990 he told me, " . . . I am doing alright, but am waiting to go back to work. I will be glad when I return to work."

After John's glasses were repaired and he was working again I went to visit him at the New River Valley Workshop. He seemed to be very happy there, and both the other workers and the staff showed real friendship toward John. He was working at the task of folding cloth shopping bags for packing and shipping. He seemed to be very proud his work. He showed me each step of the process and how important it was to make sure that it was done correctly. I remember very clearly my drive home that afternoon. I felt that finally things seemed to be coming together for John. He had a nice place to live and he was working! I also remember feeling very appreciative of the help that Diane Williamson had given to John. She was making such a difference in his life.

CAMPING WITH FRIENDS

Camp Virginia Jaycee had remained an important part of my relationship with John. Each fall and spring when I went there with my Lynchburg College students John was there as a camper. He had a special relationship with the students. Some returned every semester and looked forward to seeing him again. Other students who were new to the camp weekend experience had learned about John from the stories their friends shared with them. The story of John's no-code order had become part of the lore of the camping weekend, and John was an instant celebrity when he arrived.

In anticipation of the March camping weekend in 1991, I wrote to John in care of the staff at Fairview Home to let him know the dates. I told him that arrangements for his attendance were being worked out and that he would receive details from Camp Virginia Jaycee soon.

In early February I received a letter that John had dictated to Diane. It contained disturbing news.

> How are you Dave? I got your letter here at Fairview. I want you to come down here and see me.
>
> I can't work now because I can't see. I don't know if I can come to camp or not.
>
> ... Doctors say my eyes are bad. We will just have to wait and see about the workshop.
>
> Fairview is nice to me. I usually go to the smoking room and then to my room. It's good food here, it's *hot*. They give me some more if I ask for it. I like it alright here.
>
> I really would like to see you sometime. Please write me back soon.
> Love,
> John

FADING VISION

A few weeks earlier John's behavior and general health had changed rapidly. I learned later that he had appeared disoriented and had been wetting his pants regularly. He had also started to lash out at people again. He was hospitalized and the reason for these changes became apparent. John's vision had been very poor for a long time. Now, however, he was blind. Medical reports indicated that dramatic changes had occurred rapidly in his visual acuity. A neurologist's report included the following comments:

> ... His mental status today reveals that he is quite worried about his upcoming eye examination tomorrow and is specifically worried that he will undergo surgery and become completely blind there. He is probably legally blind in the right eye due to cloudy ocular media ...

The next day he was examined by an opthamologist. His report included, of course, greater detail about John's deteriorated vision. Among his remarks were the following observations:

Impression:

1. Blind Right Eye.
2. Corneal Dystrophy, both eyes.
3. Cataract, left eye.
4. Borderline, left eye.

For me a most telling report of the changes in John's life came through the assessment of his needs done by the registered nurse who supervised his care while he was in the hospital. Her summary comments were:

> Patient is blind-needs direction and assistance to walk and with all activities of daily living. Needs someone to light cigarettes. Generally is pleasant and cooperative. Needs food prepared for him before he begins to eat.

I was deeply disturbed by this new development in John's life. It seemed to come just when things were beginning to go well for him. He finally had a job in a good environment at the Workshop, he was living in the best adult home that I had seen, and now this. I reflected a great deal during this time about the no-code order, my questioning of it, the relationship that John and I had developed, and the seemingly endless difficulties he faced. I was confused and depressed.

John came to the weekend at Camp Virginia Jaycee in March. I tried to prepare the students for the changes that they would see in him. I explained his blindness and we talked about the possible impact that it was having on him emotionally. I was impressed with their enthusiasm over trying to make the weekend the best possible one for him given his increased need for assistance.

CARING FOR AN OLDER MAN

John's behavior over the weekend was very different than the way that he had acted at Camp Jaycee in previous years. Not only was he much more dependent on help in moving about, dressing, eating, lighting his cigarettes, and other basic things, he was also simply more sad and he seemed so much older than I had ever seen him. Camp Jaycee had always been a place where he smiled and laughed, even when things were not going well otherwise in his life. He now appeared to be just worn out, exhausted with the new disabilities he faced. He spent much of the time bent over in his chair with his head between his legs. He burned his fingers several times trying to smoke, and his counselors told me that he cried one night when he wet his pants while trying to use the urinal. He had the overall appearance of a person who was broken. I tried to remain positive in my talks with him, but I don't think I was convincing. My students once again made me so proud. They were constantly helpful and encouraging with John. Their manner with him was a beautiful blend of grandchild to grandparent, loving friend, and gentle parent. I came home after the weekend with a powerful mixture of emotions.

In May of 1991 John was declared legally blind by the Virginia Department for the Visually Handicapped. This classification made him eligible for services that would help him adapt to his visual disability. He soon began to get training to help him with mobility around Fairview. He was trained in how to find the dining room, smoking lounge, and bathroom independently. He was also given assistance in managing his room and belongings. This assistance proved to be of great help to him, both in his daily living skills and in his emotional life. As he became somewhat more independent, his morale improved.

John was also helped in his adjustment to his new circumstances by attendance at the Developmental Day Services program in the New River Valley. This program for people who are more severely disabled was the best choice for John after it was deemed no longer feasible for him to work at the Workshop. He attended Developmental Day Services for many months and enjoyed the activities there immensely.

John and I corresponded during this time on a fairly regularly basis. He always had someone write for him, and I tried to know who that person was as another point of connection with him. I sometimes wrote a note to that person on the letters that I sent to John. At times his corresponder was Diane Williamson. At other times it was someone who worked at Fairview Home.

In May 1991 John wrote a note to let me know how he was doing and to let me know that he was excited about going for a full week to Camp Virginia Jaycee during the summer. It included these comments:

> . . . It was good to hear from you. It would be great to see you in July, maybe for my birthday.
>
> I am doing better now, I have a new roommate at Fairview, we get along real good. I was also promoted to group three at the Day Program, the people in this group are nice to me.
>
> Hope to see you soon, I am excited about camp this summer.
> Sincerely,
> John

I was unable to visit John on his birthday. It came at the time my family had planned a vacation to Cape Cod, where I was also enrolled in a professional development course. I wrote to John in early July.

> I am sending you an early birthday present by Diane. You told me that what you would like most is cash so that is what you are getting. Spend it on anything you would like.

I am going to be away for a couple of weeks. I will send you a birthday card from 'up north'.

Take care of yourself. Have a great birthday!

Sincerely,

Dave

I wrote to Diane in early August. By this time she had married and her new name was Diane Eaton.

I hope this finds you well. I'm back from my trip to Massachusetts. We had a great time and I learned a lot from my course. The most exciting thing we did was a whale watch trip off of Cape Cod. We saw lots, even a mother and her calf. An unforgettable experience.

I am sending John his birth certificate as a present. Please read the enclosed note to him. It seems to me that we all should have at least small symbols of our own history. I'll try to see if I can find more for him. Please help him find a safe place in his room for this.

Take care and I hope to see you soon.

Sincerely,

Dave

I had asked John many months earlier to sign a form so that I could send for a copy of his birth certificate. As I told Diane, I felt that it was important for him to have such a simple symbol of his life. His only other life symbols were a few pictures, mostly from Camp Virginia Jaycee, a few craft projects, again from camp, and a copy of Mike Hudson's newspaper article about him.

Shortly after I wrote to Diane Eaton she called to let me know that John would soon have another case manager. Diane had decided to return to school to pursue a graduate degree in special education at Radford University. She continued to be in touch with John, however, and was a genuine friend. John also found other friends around this time. An example of this is found in a letter I wrote to him in November of 1991.

Dear John:

Thank you for your nice letter. I really enjoyed hearing from you. It was good to hear that things are going so well at Fairview. I was sorry to hear, though, that you have had a bad cold. I hope that you are better by now.

I really enjoyed seeing you at Camp Jaycee. All the Lynchburg College students liked seeing you also. Have you heard from any of them?

Enclosed is $50 to be used for cigarettes as you need them. I am asking Phyllis Bessler [an employee at Fairview] to help you with this. This money was given by the guys in a fraternity here at Lynchburg College called Sigma Mu Sigma. You know many of them from Camp Jaycee. Jim Farrell collected the money and brought it by today. It is a wonderful present and it shows how much they like you . . .

I will write you again next week to let you know when I can make my Christmas visit. I will be bringing you a small present, and we will go to lunch at McDonald's.

Take care my friend. I look forward to seeing you in a couple of weeks.

Sincerely,

Dave

MOVING

In June 1992, I moved to Columbia, South Carolina, to accept a faculty appointment at the University of South Carolina. After my move, I wrote to John regularly and talked with him occasionally on the telephone. Things seemed to continue to go well for him, and I remained convinced that Fairview was the best home that John had found since his childhood and the nurturance of his foster mother.

The case manager who took over for Diane Eaton after she left for graduate school proved to be a competent and concerned person. Her name is Mitzi Thorne. She wrote letters to me for John. She also kept me informed about her visits with him and how he was doing. Her reports tended to be cautiously optimistic. She told me on several occasions that he continued to be frustrated with the additional disabilities he was encountering because of blindness. She felt, however, that he was responding well to the individual assistance he was getting in developing techniques for being as independent as possible.

In February of 1993, however, Mitzi called with a message that was obviously difficult for her to deliver. It was also a painful one for me to receive. John was being dismissed from Fairview. Angry outbursts had once again become a common expression of his frustrations. He had been cursing, kicking, and swinging his fists at other residents and employees. Mitzi had been given notice that she would have to find another place for him to live.

Mitzi called 25 adult homes in several areas of Virginia before she found one that would take John. Each one that she called asked why he was being moved and, when told of his background with other adult homes, refused to take him. Mitzi was very candid with me about the placement she had found for John. She said that it was not like Fairview, but that it was the best she could do.

Mitzi was also distressed at what she perceived to be a personal shortcoming on her part. She felt that she had failed John. My only comfort to her was my reassurance that John's difficulties had resulted from systemic and long-standing social problems. Mitzi's efforts on John's behalf went far beyond a salary or job description. They are to be applauded.

PEOPLE WHO CAN'T PAY

My first visit to John in his new home was another lesson in the reality of the scattered pieces of purgatory that replaced many of the large centralized institutions as repositories for many of the poor, old, and damaged in our society. Burton Blatt had described his holiday visits to large mental institutions as "Christmas in Purgatory."[11] I found many of the adult homes that replaced the large institutions as simply smaller pieces of the same purgatory.

I had been given directions to the adult home by someone who assured me that I would see the entrance from the road easily as I neared it. I did, and pulled my car into a visitor space in the parking lot. The building was attractive from the outside, and as I opened one of the double doors at the front I entered a pleasant reception area. There was no receptionist at the desk. I walked down the main hall past attractively decorated rooms looking for someone who could help me find John. I saw nobody until I came to a bright dining area. A staff member came over immediately and asked if she could help me.

I explained I was there to visit John Lovelace. She looked puzzled for a moment and then said, "We don't have him here, he must be up on the hill." She took me to another door and pointed toward another, larger building. I asked her to check the records to make sure he wasn't in this building. She explained that there were only 45 people in this building and she knew them all by name. "This is a nursing home for those who can pay," she explained. "Up on the hill is the home for adults. Same name, but up there are people who can't pay." She also told me that there were 160 people living there.

I walked to the building on the hill. The attendant told me in detail how to find the door that would be unlocked. "They don't get so many visitors up there," she said. When I opened the door as directed, the overwhelming presence of cigarette smoke, urine, and disinfectant charged my senses. I was also struck by the almost startled look of staff members at the appearance of a stranger.

I asked for help, and after some confusion I was led to John's room by a woman wearing the kind of institutional uniform (white polyester pants and top, and white shoes) that today is rarely seen in "normalized" state residential facilities. My first glimpse of John was of him sitting on the edge of his bed with his head in his hands. One of his roommates was sitting on his bed rocking in an autistic fashion. Another was naked from the waist sitting in a wheelchair on a towel in excrement. I was assured that there had just been an accident.

I stayed several hours with John that day. As best as I could determine, he spent his time distributed primarily between his own room, the dining hall, and the smoking/TV room. The smoking room consisted of rows of wooden benches, floor-stand ashtrays, and a wall mounted television. It could probably accommodate 50 people. I had seen similar arrangements in other adult homes. The intensity of the smoke coming from the room into the hallway was staggering.

John was helped during his meals by one of the uniformed staff members. He seemed to eat well, and while I was there he was given patient assistance and encouragement in the dining hall. I tried to talk with those staff members who seemed most interested in John while he was having lunch. I hoped to find someone who would write letters for him. None of these people seemed to be willing to make a commitment to write for him. I suspect that the reluctance may have come from a combination of fear of becoming overly involved in a resident's life and the fact that the workers seemed already stretched to the limit by the staff-to-resident ratio. Whatever the case, however, I was unable to establish a contact among the staff.

When I wrote to John, now from South Carolina, I didn't receive a reply. When I sent him gifts there was no acknowledgement that he had received them. Between visits I had no knowledge of what was happening in his life. I often wondered if John's life was better in any way than it was on the day I met him. I also often wondered where he found the strength to survive the pain of his days.

CHAPTER 15

Policies, People, and No Room at the Graveyard

Legislation that was entitled Supplemental Security Income for the Aged, the Disabled, and the Blind was passed by the United States Congress in 1972. By the time it went into effect in 1974 it had already become known to politicians, bureaucrats, and professionals in the human services as simply SSI (Supplemental Security Income). The program provides income to all people who are eligible because of age or disability and who are, therefore, unable to enter the workforce. Although the program is fully funded with federal money, states are allowed to supplement it with additional funding for the recipients. This provision is in recognition of variations in the cost of living from state to state. Supplemental funds are provided by states only if they elect to do so. Most state supplements are relatively modest.

Although the program was designed to help individuals with disabilities, and in many cases it surely has, it was a huge stimulant to the movement toward de-institutionalization. It provided a means for states to discharge people from mental retardation and mental health institutions into communities with very little governmental cost to state budgets. Indeed, it became an attractive means for saving state money. When people were discharged from institutions into communities the daily costs to states for institutionalization were saved, and the costs of living in the community were covered largely by the federal SSI dollars. In the first few years of the existence of SSI the de-institutionalization of people with mental retardation or mental illness increased dramatically. John Lovelace was among those who left for the community during this exodus.

And so SSI made it much easier for states to de-institutionalize people, to save themselves money by doing so, and to make only minimal investments in supporting these people in their home communities. SSI does not include standards for the care and treatment of people after they leave institutions. Theoretically, the SSI benefit is paid directly to the recipient. In reality, the checks are usually signed over to adult home operators, or other providers of housing, and only a small allowance is provided for the residents. The recipients are presumed to be free to "shop" for the best living arrangements and, as such, to make the best choices for themselves in terms of care and treatment.

This free market approach to the needs of people with intellectual and developmental disabilities, however, has led to the kinds of problems discussed earlier in this book and which are clearly demonstrated through the experiences of John Lovelace. Although Virginia established a system of community services boards to provide safeguards and assistance to people with disabilities in the community, funding restraints placed severe limits on what their small professional staffs could do with large case loads. Through SSI the fiscal burden for housing people with disabilities was shifted largely to the federal level, and the involvement of the states in the care of these people was diminished. SSI came with only age and disability requirements for the recipients. It did nothing to encourage the development of quality living arrangements or meaningful community programs for these people. In fact, it encouraged the development of an industry of largely unmonitored and often substandard adult homes. The positive vision of de-institutionalization was tarnished in many cases, and in others it was made into a travesty.

HELP FROM A FRIEND

In the process of trying to be of some help to John Lovelace, and attempting to understand the meaning of his situation, I called on my friend Elliot Schewel several times. Elliot has been a businessman and public servant throughout his adult life. He was a member of the Virginia Senate for many years. In this capacity he was interested in and involved with issues of fiscal responsibility in government and the well-being of the public in other regards. He was always willing to help me find answers to questions that I posed about state government policies and practices, and he was always responsive to requests for assistance from others, which have come to him through me. He has my deepest respect and gratitude.

Elliot was willing to help me find answers to questions about the no-code order in John's case. He asked the Commissioner of Mental Health and Mental Retardation for Virginia to look into the case. The answers that were forthcoming were encouraging. There was increasing awareness of the need for protection of the rights of people with disabilities in the community. More advocates were being employed to monitor their rights and investigate possible violations. In spite of this growth, however, resources were limited for this kind of protection and the safeguards were, therefore, fragile. I believe that this was and is particularly true for people like John, who were previously institutionalized and who thereby lost contact with the family and friends who would normally have looked out for their welfare. Many of these same people were never declared incompetent during their institutionalization. They were then discharged without legal guardians and could, as John was, be called on to make profound decisions without caring assistance or legal protection.

The second time that I asked Elliot Schewel to correspond with the commissioner it concerned the overall quality of care in adult homes in Virginia. This was around the same time that Mike Hudson's series was being published. Elliot had read the series and was more than willing to inquire about what Virginia was doing to correct the situation. He pointed out to the Commissioner that even though there had been 10 years of government studies and reports on adult homes in Virginia, no action had been taken.

Elliot's inquiry brought responses that were encouraging. Efforts were being made to monitor the living conditions in adult homes. The licensing standards for these homes were becoming more rigorous, and there were increases in the services funded through Virginia's community service boards. But the bottom line remained that most of the limited money for community living for persons with intellectual disabilities came from SSI, and there were no standards and expectations under SSI for quality care, treatment, and protection for these people.

When Commissioner Howard Cullum responded to Elliot he sent a copy of a plan that he had already been working on in relation to adult homes. Commissioner Cullum was diligently seeking ways to improve the situation. He was faced, however, with the limitations of trying to deal with a problem at the state level that was tied to the national policies and practices that actually determine the possibilities for improvement and reform in services to people with disabilities.

My letter to Senator Schewel in November of 1989 after he sent me a copy of Commissioner Cullum's plan is illustrative of my sense of these limitations:

Dear Elliot:

Thanks for sending the copy of Howard Cullum's letter and his *Plan for Addressing the Needs of the Mentally Disabled Residents of Homes for Adults.* I have reviewed the plan and I believe there is a great deal of merit in what it proposes. I think that the two most important issues it speaks to are licensing and financing. The proposed plan is a move in the right direction but it seems to me that it should address more strongly and clearly the urgent need for reform in the licensing of adults homes and an increase in the financial resources provided for the care of the mentally disabled people living in these homes.

As Mike Hudson illustrated so compellingly in his *Roanoke Times and World News* series, there are essentially no teeth in the existing licensing practices for homes for adults in Virginia. It appears that obtaining a license is a simple matter. Losing a license is a rarity. There are no real penalties short of revocation. Revocation has apparently occurred only in cases of extreme and chronic violations of standards. The standards are far from being rigorous. I believe that this is a critical matter that deserves close attention.

Howard Cullum states in his letter to you that the bottom line is financial. He is absolutely correct in this observation. Most of the adult homes that Virginians with mental disabilities live in are essentially small businesses operating for profit. It is staggering to consider that these homes are expected to provide room, board, supervision, recreation and other daily needs for people who often have serious and multiple problems, all this for less than $20 per day. Somewhere in those fewer than twenty dollars, of course, a profit must be found. It is not difficult to understand, given this context, the appalling conditions and poor nutritional practices which have been found in some of these homes. The funding available for people living in adult homes in Virginia is part of a national problem that must be addressed at the federal level. As you know, support for people who were deinstitutionalized as part of the national movement did not follow people from institutions into the community. I trust that soon we will be seeing significant movement at the national level to improve the situation. I think that action must come now in Virginia, however, to do what can be done to provide a more decent level of support for people who have been largely ignored in recent years.

Elliot, I would appreciate any support you could lend to measures that would improve life for those people in Virginia who because of disabilities and other circumstances must live in adult homes. In particular, I believe that your attention to how adult homes are licensed, how they are inspected, how standards are enforced and how financial support might be increased could be of great value to these people. Thanks for taking the time to consider these comments.

Writing letters is easier than laboring within the political and financial realities that face the legislators and state administrators who are dealing with the problems that my letter articulated. Elliot Schewel and Howard Cullum continued their labors and were making a difference. In his reply to my letter Elliot concluded by saying:

> As you can see, the pace of progress is very, very slow but I am hopeful that when money becomes a little more available we will be able to make more meaningful strides to come up with solutions to these issues. That doesn't help much but it's all I can report at this time.

Indeed, it did help!

BACK TO THE INSTITUTION?

I must mention two other requests that I made to state governmental agencies that may illuminate some of the curious circumstances which were created by what was done in the name of de-institutionalization. Both were in relation to what I perceived to be John's best interests.

The first request came during one of the times when I was wondering if it was possible to find a really good place for John to live in an adult home. I had become discouraged. It appeared to me that the safeguards and services that John needed were just not available in a community setting. I came to the conclusion that he would actually be better off back in an institution. I knew that the system of resident advocacy which had been developed would insure that nothing like the no -code order would occur in a state institution. The decades of the 1970s and 1980s had brought reforms, and I was certain that a person like John would be safer inside an institution than outside. It was a startling revelation for a professor who had been lecturing and writing about the ills of institutions across those same decades!

It was with feelings of humility and great irony that I broached the subject quietly with administrators at the Central Virginia Training Center. Here I was actually asking that John be readmitted to the same institution from which he had been released 15 years earlier to a life of greater "normality" in the community. The irony and humility were short lived. I was very quickly informed that there was simply no chance that my petition for John would result in his readmission. It simply could not be done.

NO ROOM IN THE GRAVEYARD

The second request came after a conversation I had with a community services board case manager who told me about the death of man she had worked with for several years. She explained that final arrangements for people living in adult homes are often difficult to make. In many cases there is no next of kin and no resources to provide for even the most modest of burials. The possibility of a pauper's grave depends on the resources and customs of the locality in which the person dies. Cremation is sometimes the least expensive and, therefore, the most desirable alternative. She told me of the death of a man she worked with as case manager for many years after he was discharged from a state institution. When he died his remains were cremated. His ashes were delivered to her office. She still had them on a bookshelf and was not sure what to do with them. The container with his ashes had been collecting dust on her shelf for five years.

Her story disturbed me greatly and caused me to think about what would happen in the event of John's death. The idea of a completely impersonal ending to his life was difficult for me to think about.

Most of the older residential institutions in our country have their own cemeteries. I think that this is one indication of the degree to which these places became completely separated from the mainstream of society. Not only did they have walls and gates to keep people in or out, they needed their own graveyards because the ties to outside relatives had often become completely severed by the time of death of many of their residents. The graves in the cemeteries were usually identified only by a number on a metal marker. A ledger with the numbers was maintained in the administration building.

Beginning in the 1970s the metal markers at the Central Virginia Training Center were replaced with granite headstones. This gesture of respect probably went unrecognized by most people outside of the institution, but many of the longtime employees of the institution told me how much it meant to them, and to the residents. It was truly seen as a sign of respect.

The first time I visited the cemetery I was struck by the beauty of the site. It is located on several gently rolling hills and is surrounded by ancient oaks. It is the kind of place that can easily be seen as a "final resting place." It has a feeling of age and continuity to it in a strange sense. As I walked through the cemetery I thought of the changes that institutions have gone through in our country, and the various reasons people have lived, and died, in them. Carrie Buck's mother is buried there. She died the same year that I was born. I wondered what she understood of the fate of her daughter and the significance that Carrie's sterilization had for the world.

I decided that I would ask the director of the Central Virginia Training Center if arrangements could be made so that in the event of John's death he could be buried in the CVTC cemetery. I felt that if this could be arranged I could work on the other things that would be needed, such as payment for a headstone and other funeral expenses. Just having a commitment for a space in the cemetery would be comforting. With such a commitment the community services board might, I thought, be able to work with me to see that simple but decent things were provided when needed.

It seemed to me it would be an appropriate place for John when it was needed. It is not only a beautiful site but it is on the grounds of the place that was his home longer than anywhere else. I do not think that my concern with this arrangement was a morbid obsession. It just seemed like a good and reasonable matter to pursue.

The director of the Central Virginia Training Center at that time was Dr. Bill Walker. Bill had been very helpful to me in several ways. He, in fact, facilitated my access to John's files after I secured a release to review them from John. He had also been interested in some of my previous work, and I had shared a copy of the book about Carrie Buck with him. When I approached him with the idea of a plot for John in the cemetery he was open to the suggestion, and he expressed a willingness to explore it through the appropriate channels.

A few weeks later Bill was back to me with a response to the request. He said that it had been considered by the Virginia Attorney General's office and that it had been denied. The only reason that he was given was that it might set a precedent that would result in other similar requests being made, and that this might become a burden for the State. I have trouble imagining the Commonwealth of Virginia being flooded with requests for burials on the grounds of its institutions, but I let the matter drop. I did not pursue it further.

CARRIED BACK TO VIRGINIA

During my final years at the University of South Carolina, as I said earlier, I was unable to visit John very often. I continued to send small gifts and letters. I also always enclosed a stamped, self-addressed envelope along with a note that only had to be checked off telling me that he had received the money or other gifts, and that he was doing well. At first these notes were returned to me. Then they stopped. I called the adult home and was told abruptly by someone at a nursing station that there was no way to tell if John had received a gift I sent in the early fall or the Christmas present I sent to him.

I then wrote to the administrator whose name I was given when I called to inquire about the gifts. She responded to my concerns by explaining that the staff had been instructed that they were not allowed to answer any questions concerning residents. She told me that my gifts, notes, and inquiries should be sent directly to her.

For the next two years I sent money and other gifts to John through this administrator. I regularly received confirmation from her of receiving the gifts and assurance that he was doing fine. Then the confirmations and assurances stopped coming.

By this time I had moved back to Virginia to accept the position of Dean of Education and Human Services at Longwood College. After not hearing anything from or about John I went to the adult home where he was living, or at least where I thought he was living. The administrator with whom I communicated was no longer there. The person who was now in the director's office explained that John had been discharged months earlier. At first she claimed that she had no records concerning his whereabouts. After I pushed a bit she gave me the name of his social worker.

In May of that year, John had been brought to the emergency room of a hospital near Roanoke. He had injuries that were attributed to his falling down five steps. Upon close examination, however, his body was found to be covered with new and old abrasions and lacerations. His whole body was described as being very filthy. He was admitted to the hospital for treatment and Social Services was contacted. An emergency custody order was issued by a magistrate, and after several days he was transferred to Catawba Hospital, a state geriatric facility.

John's life may have actually been saved by this chain of events. Within months the adult home was under investigation for severe health care violations, including improper distribution of medications, outdated medical records, and a report of an unsupervised resident who had sexually abused other residents. The owners of the home were told that unless changes were made quickly their license would be revoked by the Virginia Department of Social Services.

While under investigation the facility experienced other problems, including the death of a resident who wandered out of the home and onto the busy highway that ran in front of it. He was struck by a car in the early morning darkness. Amazingly, the home won an appeal to remain open and only closed after the corporation that owned it declared that it was losing money on the operation.

YOU WERE A VICTIM

After he was sent to Catawba Hospital John received a letter from the Department of Social Services of Franklin County, Virginia. It explained that their investigation found that he had been a victim of abuse and neglect, and that he was in need of protective services. That need for protection may have been the reason that the rules were bent somewhat regarding his stay at Catawba. The hospital is not a long-term care facility. The regulations there called for him to be placed in a long-term facility as soon as his acute health care needs had been addressed.

When I found John at Catawba with the help of a social worker in Franklin County I immediately began to work with Robert Penn. Robert proved to be an outstanding social worker and humanitarian. He worked patiently with me and with John. He invested a great deal of time and energy in trying to find a good placement for John. What he now needed was a place in a nursing home. John was losing his hearing, he was blind, and, quite simply, he had aged rapidly from his experiences of the last few years. He looked and acted like a very elderly man.

The problem we faced at this point was that we could not find a nursing home that we could feel comfortable with as a place for John to live that was willing to accept him. The rejections that we received from the nursing homes that would have been our choices came down to one fact. John had no family members who could make decisions regarding care and treatment. If John was admitted there would be nobody to make difficult life and death decisions for him. Nursing homes would not take the risk of being in the position of having a resident that placed them in a seemingly unending commitment regardless of what might, in fact, be in the best interests of the person both medically and ethically.

The only solution to this problem was for someone to become John's legal guardian. This was the necessary condition for his having at chance to be accepted by a decent nursing care facility. I secured the assistance of a lawyer in John's hometown of Martinsville. A legal petition was prepared and on December 9 of 1999 I appeared before the Circuit Court of the City of Martinsville. On that same day I was appointed John's guardian, and I was vested with all decisions regarding medical treatment and matters of consent.

By late December John was diagnosed with pneumonia and dehydration. I was asked to approve appropriate treatment. I was also asked to approve his transfer to Richfield Nursing Center near

Roanoke. I visited Richfield and I was impressed with the care that residents there were receiving. His transfer from Catawba to Richfield was almost immediate.

A NO-CODE ORDER

In early January of 2000 I was asked by the head nurse on John's floor at Richfield to visit with her to talk about his medical condition. He had reoccurring pneumonia and he was at times aspirating food. He was often refusing nourishment. He spent most of his days sleeping. The nurse, a wonderful person named Jewel Jones, explained that the only treatment for the nourishment issue and the aspiration of food would be a feeding tube surgically inserted in his stomach. She also explained that intervention in the case of cardiac arrest would be very aggressive pressure on his chest that could break ribs and puncture his lungs. She asked that I think about what was best for John. The next day I sent the following letter to Ms. Jones.

> January 5, 2000
>
> Dear Ms. Jones:
>
> I am returning the enclosed Natural Death Act Declaration for John Lovelace that we discussed yesterday. As you will see from my signature, I have decided that this decision is in John's best interest.
>
> This was a very difficult decision for me. I have given much thought to the changes that have occurred in John's life since I have known him. As we discussed, one of my concerns on John's behalf years ago was a no code order that was executed, in my opinion, without true regard for John's value as a person. It is ironic that I now find the changes in John's health and the possible consequences of artificially prolonging his life make this the most responsible and caring decision I can make for him.
>
> I appreciate your assurances that John will receive the medical care that he needs in all circumstances, short of artificially prolonging the dying process if his death is imminent. Everything that I have seen at Richfield and my interaction with the staff convinces me that this is the case.
>
> Thank you for your help with this difficult issue in John's life. Thank you also for the care and concern you have expressed for him.
>
> Sincerely,
>
> J. David Smith

THE ENDING

John died on May 21, 2001, of aspiration pneumonia. He was 70 years old. His death certificate listed his occupation as a laborer.

Indeed, he did spend his life laboring against great odds. With the help of a local funeral director I was able to find a peaceful grave site in a hillside cemetery. Other arrangements were made with his help as well. A grave-side service was held, and my father and I were joined by Richfield staff members and a few other people who had come to care about John and to bid him farewell. A simple marker with his name, birth date, and date of death was put in place a few months later.

An irony followed almost two years after John's death. I was contacted by the daughter of John's foster sister, Mrs. Hunter's daughter. She was, of course, quite elderly. She was older than John. She had asked her own daughter to try to find John (she used the nickname "Billy" for him). Her search had led her to me, but the sources she had talked with in finding me could not give her confidential information concerning John. I had to inform her, of course, of John's passing. I talked with her about John's life after her mother lost contact with him (and he with her and the only family he had known). Within a few days she wrote to me asking for the date of his death and his place of burial. I sent this information. I wish their search for John had commenced earlier. I know their interest in him would have made him happy.

Epilogue

While I was reflecting on my experience with John Lovelace, I read an excellent book by William F. May entitled *The Patient's Ordeal*. In his introduction to the book, May describes an exchange that T. S. Eliot once had with a college student—one very much like the exchange I described at the beginning of this tale. Eliot had given a lecture on some serious problem in American life. During the question period that followed, the student asked urgently, "Mr. Eliot, what are we going to do about the problem you have discussed?" Eliot replied to the student, "You have asked the wrong question. You must understand that we face two types of problems in life. One kind of problem provokes the question 'What are we going to do about it?' The other kind poses the subtler question 'How do we behave toward it?'"[1]

It seems clear to me that the first kind of problem can be solved with direct, sometimes simple and immediate action. The immediate relief that a doctor or dentist may give a patient is an example of this kind of problem resolution. The second kind of problem is a greater challenge. This is a problem that has no direct, simple, or immediate solution. What do you do for a dying friend or family member? Do you avoid that person because you cannot cure his or her suffering or prevent the inevitable? Abiding by your friend or relative in such a situation requires a different approach to the problem: You must see it as a factor to be lived with, as part of an enduring relationship.

When I initially tried to respond to my student's question of "What are you going to do about it?" I approached John Lovelace from the first perspective. I sought a fast and clean solution to the problem of his protection and well-being. As I came to know him, however, I learned that he needed more than a "quick fix" to his problems: He needed a friend. He needed a sense of connectedness that would endure his constant changes in circumstances. I suspect that this is the greatest need of many of our fellow human beings. The simple problems that can be fixed quickly are not the ones that drain us. Having people who will endure with us is one of the greatest of our human needs.

Through coming to know John Lovelace, I gained new insights into the experience of people who have disabilities. I also came to know in much more real terms the problems of the systems supposedly designed to help these people. In my lifetime, I will be able to make, at best, only a minimal difference in these systems and what they do for people. Through coming to know John Lovelace, however, I learned more about the mysteries of human relationships. I was strengthened in my understanding that small gestures of caring, not huge heroic feats, are the essence of friendship. I learned more deeply the importance of facing suffering and unsolvable problems with other people rather than avoiding people whose problems you do not have the power to make "right."

Efforts to define disability have their foundation in the elusive concept of *normality*. There may be no better example of this concept than one from a story about the institutionalized woman whom Henry Goddard gave the pseudonym "Deborah Kallikak," as was described earlier. The Vineland State School social worker Helen Reeves reported on a conversation with Deborah:

> ... The discussion comes to an abrupt end as she suddenly remarks: "D'you know, its normal people who are the real problems. *They* think us feeble-minded people are problems, but *they're* the real ones. They got so much to think about, half the time they don't know what to think. Yessir, normal people are the real problems ... I been watching 'em a long time now!"
>
> "But, Deborah, as you know, the feeble-minded problem is considered very depressing by a lot of folks. Of course, it isn't, but what about the problem of normal people. Is that depressing?"
>
> "Sometimes yes, and sometimes no," replies Deborah, warily. "I'd say most generally always, yes."[2]

Deborah's insights on the concept of normality provide an excellent perspective on society's efforts to understand and respond to disability. Defining disability has frequently been done without input from those individuals most directly affected by those changes. The defining has been done by "normal" people. It has often been done in service of what "normal" people have deemed to be in their own best interests. Deborah's wisdom provides us with direction for the future in seeking not only self-determination for individuals with disabilities but their leadership in terms of creating a society that truly affords appropriate support and broad opportunities for all people. Perhaps if we recognize the value in people who have so often been excluded from our world, there will be less coercion and violence in it.

A final note of thanks to my friend John Lovelace. Two years following John's death at Richfield, my father passed away on the same floor of that facility. His final days were filled with pain and a struggle to maintain his dignity. I was far from being a perfect son to him during his ordeal. I was a better son, however, than I might have been without the lessons I learned through the life of my friend and his battles with "normality."

Five years ago I asserted in print that it was time to admit that the term mental retardation was a myth, a "false and unhelpful categorization of people with very diverse needs and characteristics."[3] I quoted from Thomas Ssasz's classic work, *The Myth of Mental Illness,* and I described the term mental retardation as being "scientifically worthless and socially harmful."[4] I argued that the term should become an historical artifact of our evolving thought about children and adults with developmental disabilities. In my opinion the millions of people who have been misunderstood and, sometimes, maligned by the term are deserving of a change in the manner in which they are regarded and treated. A disassembling of the aggregation of human conditions gathered under the term mental retardation might provide an opportunity to enhance our vision of who these people are as individuals and our understanding of their rightful places in our communities.[5]

More important than changing terms, however, is changing our minds about the needs and potentials of the people with the disabilities to whom the words refer. Most important is that we recognize that millions of people have had their lives diminished by the words we have used, and the lack of value we have placed on their lives. If John Lovelace's story helps us to understand the need for change in our thinking he will have left us a precious legacy.

Notes

INTRODUCTION

1. Winston Groom, *Forrest Gump* (New York: Doubleday, 1986), 1–2.

2. Eugene Doll, "Deborah Kallikak: 1889–1978, a Memorial," *Mental Retardation* 21 (winter, 1983), 30.

3. Helen Reeves, "So Depressing," *Training School Bulletin* 44 (1948), 195–196.

4. Doll, "Deborah Kallikak," 30–32.

5. Helen Reeves, "Travels with a Celebrity," *Training School Bulletin* 42 (1945), 3.

6. Doll, "Deborah Kallikak," 32.

7. Reeves, "So Depressing," 196.

8. Reeves, "So Depressing," 197.

9. Reeves, "Travels with a Celebrity," 2–3.

10. Henry Goddard, *The Kallikak Family: A Study in the Heredity of Feeble-Mindedness* (New York: MacMillan, 1912), 11–12.

11. Reeves, "So Depressing," 199.

12. Reeves, "Travels with a Celebrity," 2.

13. J. David Smith, *Minds Made Feeble: The Myth and Legacy of the Kallikaks* (Rockville: Aspen, 1985).

14. Elizabeth Cooper, *Mother, Can You Hear Me?* (New York: Dodd, Mead & Co., 1983), 79.

15. Michael D'Antonio, *The State Boys Rebellion* (New York: Simon & Schuster, 2004), 77.

16. D'Antonio, *The State Boys,* 78.

17. D'Antonio, *The State Boys,* 82–83.

18. D'Antonio, *The State Boys.*

19. Robert Haney, " 'I Care About Them,' Says Woman in Sex Abuse Case," *New York Times,* December 16, 1992, Health section.

20. Bernard Lefkowitz, *Our Guys* (New York: Vantage, 1997), 162.

21. Steven Gelb, "The Problem of Typological Thinking in Mental Retardation," *Mental Retardation* 35 (winter 1997), 448–57.

22. Sarah Triano and Laura Obara, "Coming Home to Disabled Country," American Association of People with Disabilities, http://www.aapd-dc.org.

23. Triano and Obara, "Coming Home."
24. Triano and Obara, "Coming Home."

CHAPTER 2

1. Judith Thomson, "A Defense of Abortion," *Philosophy and Public Affairs* 1 (Fall, 1971), 47–66.

CHAPTER 3

1. J. David Smith, *The Eugenic Assault on America: Scenes in Red, White and Black* (Fairfax: George Mason University Press, 1993).
2. Adolf Hitler, *Mein Kampf* (Boston: Houghton Mifflin, 1971), 255.
3. J. David Smith and Ray Nelson, *The Sterilization of Carrie Buck* (Far Hills: New Horizon Press, 1989).

CHAPTER 4

1. James Trent, *Inventing the Feeble Mind: A History of Mental Retardation in the United States* (Berkeley: University of California Press, 1994).
2. Iona Opie and Peter Opie, *The Oxford Dictionary of Nursery Rhymes* (Oxford: Oxford University Press, 1951), 385.
3. Philip Ferguson, *Abandoned to Their Fate: Social Policy and the Practice Toward Severely Retarded People America, 1820–1920* (Philadelphia: Temple University Press, 1994), 16.

CHAPTER 5

1. Ralph Ellison, *Invisible Man* (New York: Random House, 1952), 2.
2. Ellison, *Invisible Man*, 3.

CHAPTER 6

1. Jack London, "Told in the Drooling Ward," in *The Turtles of Tasman* (New York: MacMillan, 1916), 87.
2. London, "Drooling Ward," 88.
3. London, "Drooling Ward," 90.

CHAPTER 7

1. Edward Bellamy, *Looking Backward* (New York: Ticknor, 1888), 178.
2. Bellamy, *Looking Backward*, 181.
3. James Watson, "Looking Forward," *Gene* 135 (Winter 1993), 314.

4. Watson, "Looking Forward," 315.

5. James Watson, *Stupid Should Be Cured, Says DNA Discoverer* (New York: NewScientist.com. Reed Business Information, 2003), 16.

6. James Watson, *Genetic Polymorphism and the Surrounding Environment in Human Genome Project: Ethics* (Madrid, Spain: BBV, 1992), 16.

7. James Watson, *1996 Annual Report, President's Essay* (Cold Spring Harbor: Cold Spring Harbor Laboratory, 1996), 15.

8. Watson, "President's Essay," 14.

9. Watson, *Stupid Should Be Cured*, 1.

10. Troy Duster, *Backdoor to Eugenics* (New York: Routledge, 1990).

11. J. David Smith, *Pieces of Purgatory: Mental Retardation In and Out of Institutions* (Pacific Grove: Brooks/Cole, 1995), 61–62.

12. U.S. House of Representatives Select Committee on Aging, *Board and Care Homes in America: A National Tragedy* (Washington DC: Author, 1989).

CHAPTER 9

1. Winston Groom, *Forrest Gump* (New York: Doubleday, 1986), 41.

2. J. David Smith, *Minds Made Feeble: The Myth and Legacy of the Kallikaks* (Rockville: Aspen Press, 1985).

3. Henry Goddard, *Human Efficiency and Levels of Intelligence* (Princeton: Princeton University Press, 1920).

4. George Bliss, "Mental Defectives and the War," *Journal of Psycho-Asthenics* 24, (1919):11–17.

5. Bliss, "Mental Defectives," 11–17.

6. Richard Scheerenberger, *A History of Mental Retardation* (Baltimore: Brookes, 1983).

7. Smith, *Minds Made Feeble.*

8. James Trent, *Inventing the Feeble Mind: A History of Mental Retardation in the United States* (Berkeley: University of California Press, 1994).

9. Edgar Doll, "Notes on the Concept of Mental Deficiency," *American Journal of Psychology* 54 (1941), 116–124.

10. Stephen Gelb, "Mental Deficients' Fighting Fascism: The Unplanned Normalization of World War 11," in *Mental Retardation in America*, ed. Steven Noll and James Trent (New York: New York University Press, 2004), 308–321.

11. Gelb, "Mental Deficients," 308–321.

12. William C. Menninger, "The Problem of the Mentally Retarded and the Army," *American Journal of Mental Deficiency* 48 (1943), 55–61.

13. Gelb, "Mental Deficients," 308–321.

14. Rebecca McKeon, "Mentally Retarded Boys in War Time," *Mental Hygiene* 30 (1946), 55.

15. Edgar Doll, "Mental Defectives and the War," *American Journal of Mental Deficiency* 49 (1944), 66.

16. Harold H. Ramsey, "How the High-Grade Mentally Defective May Help in the Prosecution of War," *American Journal of Mental Deficiency* 47 (1942), 78.

17. E. Arthur Whitney and E. Mildred MacIntyre, "War Record of Elwyn Boys," *American Journal of Mental Deficiency* 49 (1944), 82.

18. Whitney and McIntyre, "War Record of Elwyn Boys," 82.

19. Thomas R. Weaver, "The Incident of Maladjustment Among Mental Defectives in Military Environment," *American Journal of Mental Deficiency* 51 (1946), 245.

20. Weaver, "Incident of Maladjustment," 246.

21. Smith, *Minds Made Feeble.*

22. Joseph Mastin, "The New Colony Plans for the Feebleminded," *Journal of Psycho-Asthenics* 21 (1916), 25–35.

23. Smith, *Minds Made Feeble.*

24. J. David Smith and Edward A. Polloway, "Patterns of Deinstitutionalization and Community Placement," *Education and Training in Mental Retardation and Developmental Disabilities* 30 (1995), 327–328.

25. Smith and Polloway, "Patterns of Deinstitutionalization and Community Placement," 325.

CHAPTER 10

1. J. David Smith, *Minds Made Feeble: The Myth and Legacy of the Kallikaks* (Austin, TX: Pro Ed, 1985).

2. Edwin Black, *War Against the Weak: Eugenics and America's Campaign to Create a Master Race* (New York: Four Walls Eight Windows, 2003).

3. Norm Ledgin, *Diagnosing Jefferson: Evidence of a Condition that Guided His Beliefs, Behavior, and Personal Associations* (Arlington, TX: Future Horizons, 2000), 44.

4. Ledgin, *Diagnosing Jefferson,* 44.

5. Ledgin, *Diagnosing Jefferson,* 45.

6. Ledgin, *Diagnosing Jefferson.*

7. Ledgin, *Diagnosing Jefferson,* 27.

8. Ledgin, *Diagnosing Jefferson,* 58.

9. Fawn Brodie, *Thomas Jefferson: An Intimate Biography* (New York: W. W. Norton, 1974).

10. Alf Mapp, *Thomas Jefferson: A Strange Case of Mistaken Identity* (Latham, MD: Madison Books, 1987).

11. Sarah Randolph, *The Domestic Life of Thomas Jefferson* (New York: Frederick Ungar Publishing, 1958).

12. Brodie, *Thomas Jefferson: An Intimate Biography.*

13. Brodie, *Thomas Jefferson: An Intimate Biography.*

14. Brodie, *Thomas Jefferson: An Intimate Biography,* 71.

15. Penny Richards and George Singer, " 'To Draw Out the Effort of His Mind': Educating a Child with Mental Retardation in Early Nineteenth-Century America," *The Journal of Special Education* 31 (1998), 443–466.

16. Page Smith, *Jefferson: A Revealing Biography* (New York: American Heritage, 1976).

17. Norman K. Risjord, *Thomas Jefferson* (Madison, WI: Madison House, 1994).

18. Richards and Singer, "To Draw Out the Effort," 5.

19. Dumas Malone, *The Sage of Monticello* (Boston: Little Brown, 1981).

20. Deposition of September 15, 1815 (Carr-Cary Papers, UVA), quoted in Dumas Malone, *The Sage of Monticello* (Boston: Little Brown, 1981), 155.

21. Bernard Mayo, *Thomas Jefferson and His Unknown Brother* (Charlottesville, VA, 1942), quoted in James A. Bear, editor, *Jefferson at Monticello* (Charlottesville, VA: University Press of Virginia, 1967), 22.

22. Eyler R. Coates, *The Jefferson-Hemings Myth: An American Travesty* (Charlottesville, VA: Thomas Jefferson Heritage Society, 2001), 93.

23. Rebecca Lee McMurry, Paternity of Sally Heming's Children, Herbert Barger, Jefferson Family Historian, http://www.angelfire.com/va/TJTruth/mcmurry3.html (accessed July 11, 2006).

24. Parnell Wickham, "Idiocy in Virginia, 1660–1860," *Bulletin of the History of Medicine* 80 (2006), 677–701.

25. John H. Bell, *Report of the Virginia State Epileptic Colony* (Richmond, VA: Virginia State Epileptic Colony, Division of Purchasing and Printing).

CHAPTER 11

1. Charles Darwin, *The Descent of Man* (London: Murray, 1871).

2. John Langdon Down, "Observations on an Ethnic Classification of Idiots" (1866) repr. in *Perspectives in Mental Retardation*, Thomas E. Jordan (Carbondale: Southern Illinois University Press, 1966), 259–262.

3. Lewis Thomas, *The Medusa and the Snail* (New York: Viking Press, 1979).

4. Michael Merleau-Ponty, *Phenomenology of Perception* (London: Routledge & Kegan Paul, 1962).

5. Charles Darwin, "The Death of Charles Waring Darwin," in vol. 7 of *The Correspondence of Charles Darwin*, ed. Frederick Burkhardt and Sydney Smith (New York: Cambridge University Press, 1985).

6. Darwin, "The Death."

7. Simi Linton, *Claiming Disability: Knowledge and Identity* (New York: New York University Press, 1998).

8. Oliver Sacks, *Awakenings* (New York: Dutton, 1983).

CHAPTER 12

1. Adam Hochschild, "Changing Colors," *Mother Jones,* May/June 1994, 29.

2. Hochschild, "Changing Colors," 34.

3. Eldridge Cleaver, *Soul on Ice* (New York: McGraw-Hill, 1968).

4. Eldridge Cleaver, "Eldridge Cleaver Speaks Out," *TASH Newsletter* 22 (Fall 1993), 5.

5. Cleaver, "Edlridge Cleaver," 7.

6. Wolf Wolfensberger, "Common Assets of Mentally Retarded People That Are Not Commonly Acknowledged," *Mental Retardation* 26 (1988), 63–70.

7. Christopher deVinck, *The Power of the Powerless* (New York: Doubleday, 1988).

8. deVinck, *The Power,* 12.

CHAPTER 13

1. Howard Howe, "Antibody Response of Chimpanzees and Human Beings to Formalin Inactivated Trivalent Poliomyelitis Vaccine," *American Journal of Hygiene* 55 (1952), 265.

2. Howe, "Antibody Response," 275.

3. Allan Chase, *Magic Shots: A Human and Scientific Account of the Long and Continuing Struggle to Eradicate Infectious Diseases by Vaccination* (New York: William Morrow and Company, 1982).

4. Chase, *Magic Shots,* 296.

5. Hilary Koprowski, George A. Jervis, and Thomas W. Norton, "Immune Response in Human Volunteers Upon Oral Administration of a Rodent Adapted Strain of Poliomyelitis Virus," *American Journal of Hygiene* 55 (1952), 108.

6. Irena Koprowski, *A Woman Wanders Through Life and Science* (Albany: State University of New York Press, 1997), 298.

7. Koprowski, *A Woman Wonders,* 299.

8. Editorial, "Poliomyelitis: A New Approach," *Lancet* 1, i (1952), 552.

9. Hilary Koprowski, George A. Jervis, and Thomas W. Norton, "Clinical Investigation on Attenuated Strains of Poliomyelitis Virus: Use as a Method of Immunization of Children with Living Virus," *Journal of the American Medical Association* 160 (1956), 959.

10. Scott Allen, "Radiation Used on Retarded: Post War Experiments Done at Fernald School," *The Boston Globe,* December 26, 1993.

11. Scott Allen, "MIT Records Show Wider Radioactive Testing at Fernald," *The Boston Globe,* December 31, 1993.

12. Humane Society. n.d. *Humane Vivisection: Foundlings Cheaper Than Animals* (Washington, DC: Humane Society) cited in Michael Grodin and

Leonard Glantz, *Children as Research Subjects* (New York: Oxford Press, 1994).

13. John Robertson, "Dilemma in Danville," *The Hastings Center Report* II, no. 5 (October 1981), 5–8.

14. James Childress, "Protecting Handicapped Newborns: Who's In Charge and Who Pays?" in *Genetics and the Law III*, ed. Aubrey Milunsky and George J. Annas (New York: Plenum Press, 1985), 271–287.

15. Childress, "Protecting Newborns."

16. Raymond S. Duff and A. G. M Campbell, "Moral and Ethical Dilemmas in the Special Care Nursery," *The New England Journal of Medicine* 289 (October 1978), 890–894.

17. A. G. M. Campbell, "Which Infants Should Not Receive Intensive Care?" *Archives of Childhood Disease* 57 (1982), 569.

18. Stephen Wall and John Partridge, "Death in the Intensive Care Nursery: Physician Practice of Withholding Life Support," *Pediatrics* 99, no. 1 (January 1997), 64–70.

19. Joseph Fletcher, *Humanhood: Essays in Biomedical Ethics* (Buffalo, NY: Prometheus Books, 1979).

20. Wolf Wolfensberger, "Common Assets of Mentally Retarded People That Are Not Commonly Acknowledged," *Mental Retardation* 26, no. 2 (1988), 63–70.

21. Frank Clark, "Baby Doe Rules Have Been Interpreted and Applied By an Appellate Court," *Pediatrics* 116, no. 2 (August 2005).

22. Armand Matheny Antommaria, " 'Who Should Survive?': One of the Choices on Our Conscience': Mental Retardation and the History of Contemporary Bioethics," *Kennedy Institute of Ethics Journal* 16, no. 3 (2006), 205–224.

23. American Association on Intellectual and Developmental Disabilities, "Position Statement: Health Care," adopted by the Board of Directors, May 28, 2002.

24. American Association on Mental Retardation, "Resolution on 'Baby Doe' Cases," *Mental Retardation* 21 (1983), 173.

25. J. David Smith, "On the Right of Children with Mental Retardation to Life Sustaining Medical Care and Treatment," *Education and Training in Mental Retardation* 24, no. 1 (March 1989).

26. Smith, "On the Right of Children with Mental Retardation to Life Sustaining Medical Care and Treatment."

27. H. Rud Turnbull, *Consent Handbook*, American Association on Mental Deficiency (Washington, DC, 1977).

28. Turnbull, *Consent Handbook*.

29. Turnbull, *Consent Handbook*.

30. Manuel Roig-Franzia, "Long Legal Battle Over as Schiavo Dies," *Washington Post*, April 1, 2005.

CHAPTER 14

1. James Trent, *Inventing the Feeble Mind: A History of Mental Retardation in the United States* (Berkeley: University of California Press, 1995).

2. Joseph Lash, *Helen and Teacher: The Story of Helen Keller and Anne Sullivan Macy* (New York: Oxford University Press, 1980).

3. Helen Keller to Alexander Graham Bell, 5 July 1918. Alexander Graham Bell Collection, Library of Congress.

4. Burton Blatt, "Friendly Letters on the Correspondence of Helen Keller, Anne Sullivan, and Alexander Graham Bell," *Exceptional Children* 51 (1985), 405–409.

5. Burton Blatt, *In and Out of the University; Essays on Higher and Special Education* (Austin, TX: Pro-Ed, 1982).

6. Martin Pernick, *The Black Stork: Eugenics and the Death of "Defective" Babies in American Medicine and Motion Pictures Since 1915* (New York: Oxford University Press, 1980).

7. Pernick, *The Black Stork*.

8. Burton Blatt, *The Conquest of Mental Retardation* (Austin, TX: Pro-Ed, 1987).

9. Blatt, "Friendly Letters," 409.

10. Blatt, *The Conquest*.

11. Burton Blatt and Fred Kaplan, *Christmas in Purgatory: A Photographic Essay on Mental Retardation* (Boston: Allyn and Bacon, 1996).

EPILOGUE

1. William May, *The Patient's Ordeal* (Indianapolis: Indiana University Press, 1991), 3.

2. Helen Reeves. "So Depressing," *Training School Bulletin* 44 (1945), 3.

3. J. David Smith, "The Myth of Mental Retardation: Paradigm Shifts, Disaggregation, and Developmental Disabilities," *Mental Retardation*, 40, no. 1 (2002), 62–64.

4. Thomas Ssasz, *The Myth of Mental Illness: Foundations of a Theory of Personal Conduct* (New York: Harper, 1960).

5. Smith, "The Myth."

Bibliography

Alexander Graham Bell Collection, Library of Congress. Helen Keller to Alexander Graham Bell.

Allen, Scott. "MIT Records Show Wider Radioactive Testing at Fernald," *The Boston Globe*, December 31, 1993.

———. "Radiation Used on Retarded: Post War Experiments Done at Fernald School," *The Boston Globe*, December 26, 1993.

American Association on Intellectual and Developmental Disabilities. "Position Statement: Health Care," adopted by the Board of Directors, May 28, 2002.

American Association on Mental Retardation. "Resolution on 'Baby Doe' Cases." *Mental Retardation* 21 (1983): 173.

Antommaria, Armand Matheny. " 'Who Should Survive?: One of the Choices on Our Conscience:' Mental Retardation and the History of Contemporary Bioethics." *Kennedy Institute of Ethics Journal* 16, no. 3 (2006): 205–224.

Bell, John H. *Report of the Virginia State Epileptic Colony.* Richmond, VA: Virginia State Epileptic Colony, Division of Purchasing and Printing.

Bellamy, Edward. *Looking Backward.* New York: Ticknor, 1888.

Black, Edwin. *War Against the Weak: Eugenics and America's Campaign to Create a Master Race.* New York: Four Walls Eight Windows, 2003.

Blatt, Burton. *The Conquest of Mental Retardation.* Austin, TX: Pro-Ed, 1987.

———. "Friendly Letters on the Correspondence of Helen Keller, Anne Sullivan, and Alexander Graham Bell." *Exceptional Children* 51 (1985): 405–409.

———. *In and Out of the University: Essays on Higher and Special Education.* Austin, TX: Pro-Ed, 1982.

Blatt, Burton and Fred Kaplan, *Christmas in Purgatory: A Photographic Essay on Mental Retardation.* Boston: Allyn and Bacon, 1996.

Bliss, George. "Mental Defectives and the War." *Journal of Psycho-Asthenics* 24 (1919), 11–17.

Brodie, Fawn. *Thomas Jefferson: An Intimate Biography.* New York: W. W. Norton, 1974.

Campbell, A. G. M. "Which Infants Should Not Receive Intensive Care?," *Archives of Childhood Disease* 57 (1982): 569.

Chase, Allan. *Magic Shots: A Human and Scientific Account of the Long and Continuing Struggle to Eradicate Infectious Diseases by Vaccination.* New York: William Morrow and Company, 1982.

Childress, James. "Protecting Handicapped Newborns: Who's In Charge and Who Pays?" in *Genetics and the Law III,* ed. Aubrey Milunsky and George J. Annas (New York: Plenum Press, 1985), 271–287.

Clark, Frank. "Baby Doe Rules Have Been Interpreted and Applied By an Appellate Court," *Pediatrics* 116, no. 2 (August 2005).

Cleaver, Eldridge. "Eldridge Cleaver Speaks Out." *TASH Newsletter* 22 (Fall 1993), 5.

———. *Soul on Ice.* New York: McGraw-Hill, 1968.

Coates, Eyler R. *The Jefferson-Hemings Myth: An American Travesty.* Charlottesville, VA: Thomas Jefferson Heritage Society, 2001.

Cooper, Elizabeth. *Mother, Can You Hear Me?* New York: Dodd, Mead & Co., 1983.

D'Antonio, Michael. *The State Boys Rebellion.* New York: Simon & Schuster, 2004.

Darwin, Charles. "The Death of Charles Waring Darwin." In vol. 7 of *The Correspondence of Charles Darwin,* eds. Frederick Burkhardt and Sydney Smith, New York: Cambridge University Press, 1985.

———. *The Descent of Man.* London: Murray, 1871.

Deposition of September 15, 1815 (Carr-Cary Papers, UVA). Quoted in Dumas Malone, *The Sage of Monticello.* Boston: Little Brown, 1981, 155.

deVinck, Christopher. *The Power of the Powerless.* New York: Doubleday, 1988.

Doll, Edgar. "Notes on the Concept of Mental Deficiency." *American Journal of Psychology* 54 (1941): 116–124.

Doll, Eugene "Deborah Kallikak: 1889–1978, a Memorial." *Mental Retardation* 21 (winter, 1983).

Down, John Langdon. "Observations on an Ethnic Classification of Idiots." 1866. Reprinted in *Perspectives in Mental Retardation,* Thomas E. Jordan. Carbondale: Southern Illinois University Press, 1966.

Duff, Raymond S. and A. G. M Campbell, "Moral and Ethical Dilemmas in the Special Care Nursery," *The New England Journal of Medicine* 289 (October 1978): 890–894.

Duster, Troy. *Backdoor to Eugenics.* New York: Routledge, 1990.

Editorial. "Poliomyelitis: A New Approach," *Lancet* 1, i (1952): 552.

Ellison, Ralph. *Invisible Man.* New York: Random House, 1952.

Ferguson, Philip. *Abandoned to Their Fate: Social Policy and the Practice Toward Severely Retarded People America, 1820–1920.* Philadelphia: Temple University Press, 1994.

Fletcher, Joseph. *Humanhood: Essays in Biomedical Ethics.* Buffalo, NY: Prometheus Books, 1979.

Gelb, Stephen. " 'Mental Deficients' Fighting Fascism: The Unplanned Normalization of World War 11." *Mental Retardation in America,* ed. Steven Noll and James Trent, 308–321. New York: New York University Press, 2004.

Gelb, Steven. "The Problem of Typological Thinking in Mental Retardation." *Mental Retardation* 35 (winter 1997): 448–57.

Goddard, Henry. *Human Efficiency and Levels of Intelligence.* Princeton: Princeton University Press, 1920.

———. *The Kallikak family: A Study in the Heredity of Feeble-Mindedness.* New York: MacMillan, 1912.

Groom, Winston. *Forrest Gump.* New York: Doubleday, 1986.

Haney, Robert. " 'I Care About Them,' Says Woman in Sex Abuse Case." *New York Times,* December 16, 1992, Health section.

Hitler, Adolf. *Mein Kampf.* Boston: Houghton Mifflin, 1971.

Hochschild, Adam. "Changing Colors." *Mother Jones,* May/June 1994, 29.

Howe, Howard. "Antibody Response of Chimpanzees and Human Beings to Formalin Inactivated Trivalent Poliomyelitis Vaccine." *American Journal of Hygiene* 55 (1952): 265.

Hubbel, Hiram. "Mental Defectives in the Armed Services." *American Journal of Mental Deficiency* 50 (1945): 137.

Humane Society. n.d. *Humane Vivisection: Foundlings Cheaper Than Animals* (Washington, D.C.: Humane Society) cited in Michael Grodin and Leonard Glantz, *Children as Research Subjects* (New York: Oxford Press, 1994).

Koprowska, Irena. *A Woman Wanders Through Life and Science.* Albany: State University of New York Press, 1997.

Koprowski, Hilary, George A. Jervis, and Thomas W. Norton, "Clinical Investigation on Attenuated Strains of Poliomyelitis Virus: Use as a Method of Immunization of Children with Living Virus," *Journal of the American Medical Association* 160 (1956): 959.

———. "Immune Response in Human Volunteers Upon Oral Administration of a Rodent Adapted Strain of Poliomyelitis Virus." *American Journal of Hygiene* 55 (1952): 108.

Lash, Joseph. *Helen and Teacher: The Story of Helen Keller and Anne Sullivan Macy.* New York: Oxford University Press, 1980.

Ledgin, Norm. *Diagnosing Jefferson: Evidence of a Condition that Guided His Beliefs, Behavior, and Personal Associations.* Arlington, TX: Future Horizons, 2000.

Lefkowitz, Bernard. *Our Guys.* New York: Vantage, 1997.

Linton, Simi. *Claiming Disability: Knowledge and Identity.* New York: New York University Press, 1998.

London, Jack. "Told in the Drooling Ward." *The Turtles of Tasman.* New York: MacMillan, 1916, 87.

Malone, Dumas. *The Sage of Monticello.* Boston: Little Brown, 1981.

Mapp, Alf. *Thomas Jefferson: A Strange Case of Mistaken Identity.* Latham, MD: Madison Books, 1987.

Mastin, Joseph. "The New Colony Plans for the Feebleminded." *Journal of Psycho-Asthenics* 21 (1916): 25–35.

May, William. *The Patient's Ordeal.* Indianapolis: Indiana University Press, 1991.

Mayo, Bernard. *Thomas Jefferson and His Unknown Brother.* Charlottesville, VA., 1942. Quoted in James A. Bear, ed., *Jefferson at Monticello.* Charlottesville, VA: University Press of Virginia, 1967.

McKeon, Rebecca. "Mentally Retarded Boys in War Time." *Mental Hygiene* 30 (1946): 55.

McMurry, Rebecca Lee. "Paternity of Sally Heming's Children, Statement of Rebecca Lee McMurry." Thomas Jefferson–Sally Hemings DNA Study. http://www.angelfire.com/va/TJTruth/mcmurry3.html (accessed July 11, 2006).

Menninger, William C. "The Problem of the Mentally Retarded and the Army." *American Journal of Mental Deficiency* 48 (1943): 55–61.

Merleau-Ponty, Michael. *Phenomenology of Perception.* London: Routledge & Kegan Paul, 1962.

Opie, Iona and Peter Opie. *The Oxford Dictionary of Nursery Rhymes.* Oxford: Oxford University Press, 1951.

Pernick, Martin. *The Black Stork: Eugenics and the Death of "Defective" Babies in American Medicine and Motion Pictures Since 1915.* New York: Oxford University Press, 1980.

Ramsey, Harold H. "How the High-Grade Mentally Defective May Help in the Prosecution of War." *American Journal of Mental Deficiency* 47 (1942): 78.

Randolph, Sarah. *The Domestic Life of Thomas Jefferson.* New York: Frederick Ungar Publishing, 1958.

Reeves, Helen. "So Depressing." *Training School Bulletin* 44 (1948): 195–196.

———. "Travels with a Celebrity." *Training School Bulletin* 42 (1945): 3.

Richards, Penny and George Singer, " 'To Draw Out the Effort of His Mind:' Educating a Child with Mental Retardation in Early Nineteenth-Century America," *The Journal of Special Education* 31 (1998): 443–466.

Risjord, Norman K. *Thomas Jefferson.* Madison, WI: Madison House, 1994.

Robertson, John. "Dilemma in Danville," *The Hastings Center Report* II, no. 5 (October 1981): 5–8.

Roig-Franzia, Manuel. "Long Legal Battle Over as Schiavo Dies," *Washington Post,* April 1, 2005.

Sacks, Oliver. *Awakenings.* New York: Dutton, 1983.

Scheerenberger, Richard. *A History of Mental Retardation.* Baltimore: Brookes, 1983.

Smith, David J. *The Eugenic Assault on America: Scenes in Red, White and Black.* Fairfax: George Mason University Press, 1993.

———. *Minds Made Feeble: The Myth and Legacy of the Kallikaks.* Rockville: Aspen, 1985.

———. "The Myth of Mental Retardation: Paradigm Shifts, Disaggregation, and Developmental Disabilities." *Mental Retardation,* 40, no. 1 (2002): 62–64.

————. "On the Right of Children with Mental Retardation to Life Sustaining Medical Care and Treatment," *Education and Training in Mental Retardation* 24, no.1 (March 1989).

————. *Pieces of Purgatory: Mental Retardation In and Out of Institutions.* Pacific Grove: Brooks/Cole, 1995.

Smith, David J. and Edward A. Polloway. "Patterns of Deinstitutionalization and Community Placement." *Education and Training in Mental Retardation and Developmental Disabilities* 30 (1995): 327–328.

Smith, David J. and Ray Nelson, *The Sterilization of Carrie Buck.* Far Hills: New Horizon Press, 1989.

Smith, Page. *Jefferson: A Revealing Biography.* New York: American Heritage, 1976.

Ssasz, Thomas. *The Myth of Mental Illness: Foundations of a Theory of Personal Conduct.* New York: Harper, 1960.

Thomas, Lewis. *The Medusa and the Snail.* New York: Viking Press, 1979.

Thomson, Judith. "A Defense of Abortion." *Philosophy and Public Affairs* 1, (Fall, 1971): 47–66.

Trent, James. *Inventing the Feeble Mind: A History of Mental Retardation in the United States.* Berkeley: University of California Press, 1994.

Triano, Sarah and Laura Obara. "Coming Home to Disabled Country." American Association of People with Disabilities, http://www.aapd-dc.org.

Turnbull, Rud H. Consent Handbook, *American Association on Mental Deficiency.* Washington, D.C., 1977.

U.S. House of Representatives Select Committee on Aging, *Board and Care Homes in America: A National Tragedy.* Washington D.C.: Author, 1989.

Wall, Stephen and John Partridge. "Death in the Intensive Care Nursery: Physician Practice of Withholding Life Support," *Pediatrics* 99, no.1 (January 1997): 64–70.

Watson, James. *1996 Annual Report, President's Essay.* Cold Spring Harbor: Cold Spring Harbor Laboratory, 1996.

————. *Genetic Polymorphism and the Surrounding Environment in Human Genome Project: Ethics.* Madrid, Spain: BBV, 1992.

————. "Looking Forward." *Gene* 135 (Winter 1993): 314.

————. *Stupid Should Be Cured, Says DNA Discoverer.* New York: NewScientist.com. Reed Business Information, 2003.

Weaver, Thomas R. "The Incident of Maladjustment Among Mental Defectives in Military Environment." *American Journal of Mental Deficiency* 51 (1946): 245.

Whitney, Arthur E. and E. Mildred MacIntyre. "War Record of Elwyn Boys." *American Journal of Mental Deficiency* 49 (1944): 82.

Wickham, Parnell. "Idiocy in Virginia, 1660–1860," *Bulletin of the History of Medicine* 80 (2006): 677–701.

Wolfensberger, Wolf. "Common Assets of Mentally Retarded People That Are Not Commonly Acknowledged." *Mental Retardation* 26 (1988), 63–70.

Index

About the Author

J. DAVID SMITH is Professor of Special Education and Chair of the Department of Specialized Education Services at the University of North Carolina at Greensboro. Smith is the author of 13 books. One of the integrating themes of his research and writing has been a concern for the rights and dignity of people with disabilities. He also has a particular interest in the history of intellectual and developmental disabilities.